SECOND EDITION

Evaluating Programs
to Increase
Student Achievement

SECOND EDITION

Evaluating Programs to Increase Student Achievement

Martin H. Jason

Foreword by **Cozette Buckney**

CORWIN PRESS
A SAGE Company
Thousand Oaks, CA 91320

For information:

Corwin Press, Inc.
A SAGE Company
2455 Teller Road
Thousand Oaks, California 91320
www.corwinpress.com

SAGE India Pvt. Ltd.
B 1/I 1 Mohan Cooperative
Industrial Area
Mathura Road, New Delhi 110 044
India

SAGE Ltd.
1 Oliver's Yard
55 City Road
London, EC1Y 1SP
United Kingdom

SAGE Asia-Pacific Pte. Ltd.
33 Pekin Street #02-01
Far East Square
Singapore 048763

Printed in the United States of America

Library of Congress Cataloging-in-Publication Data

Jason, Martin H.
  Evaluating programs to increase student achievement / Martin H. Jason.
— 2nd ed.
    p. cm.
  Includes bibliographical references and index.
ISBN 978-1-4129-5124-1 (cloth)
ISBN 978-1-4129-5125-8 (pbk.)
  1. Educational evaluation. 2. School management and organization. 3. Academic achievement. I. Title.

  LB2822.75.J37 2008
  379.1'58—dc22

                                                                    2007040297

This book is printed on acid-free paper.

08 09 10 11 10 9 8 7 6 5 4 3 2 1

Acquisitions Editor: Cathy Hernandez
Editorial Assistants: Megan Bedell & Ena Rosen
Production Editor: Appingo Publishing Services
Cover Designer: Lisa Riley

Contents

Foreword

Five years ago, I had the privilege of writing the foreword to the 1st edition of this book. I felt then, as I do now, that principals need all the tools available to help them make needed programmatic decisions to enhance their students' achievement.

This concept is even more relevant today with the constant pressure of the No Child Left Behind (NCLB) Act. State and local school boards of education are expecting schools to often make huge leaps in test scores while offering little in the way of supporting information on how to accomplish that feat. Education vendors have become a cottage industry, creating numerous programs designed to improve student achievement and raise test scores. Without some way to determine what is, or is not, working in their school, principals are subject to almost "snake oil like" sales promises.

Additionally, as schools move toward shared decision making and team leadership models, those persons need direction in determining the programs they currently, or propose to, use to meet their educational goals. This book provides them with that direction.

In this assessment age of education, data is gathered and constantly sent to teachers, parents, principals, and school board members. Too often this information is received and then set upon a shelf because persons do not understand how that data, along with other information, can be used to improve student achievement. This book provides those tools.

A step-by-step guide is presented to assist even the most novice school leader in determining how to analyze their school's academic programs. Evaluation cannot be done in isolation and this book helps leaders view their academic programs in light of the entire school organization and goals for improvement.

Additionally, concepts such as validity and reliability are discussed in a manner that is clearly written and easily understood. The six phases of the evaluation process, as identified by the author, are detailed and supported with easily understandable graphs and charts.

The book ends with a guide to help principals more fully understand their role as a leader in the process of school improvement and program evaluation. The author emphasizes the "multidimensional responsibilities of the principal in program evaluation" with a principal assessment form that will prove valuable in making those crucial decisions.

Since the 2003 edition, I have worked in Philadelphia and St. Louis, and am currently with the Recovery School District of New Orleans, helping superintendents create an improved learning environment. One concern has been constant in each of these struggling school districts—how to select the best academic programs for improving student achievement.

I am proud to say, reading this book will go a long way toward answering that question.

Cozette Buckney, EdD
Adjunct to Roosevelt University
Executive Director for the Institute of Education Services and
    Academic Achievement
Executive Assistant to the Superintendent of the New Orleans
    Recovery School District

Preface

Although this book provides practical guidelines that personnel in an individual school can follow in evaluating programs, it is fundamentally a book about winning. This perspective is consistent with a need identified by Sergiovanni (1984) for students and staff to "experience success [and] think of themselves as winners" (p. 13).

The current emphasis on test results as the single most important indicator of a school's effectiveness heightens the need for students, administrators, and staff to feel the pride that accompanies winning. Carrying out program evaluations can help meet this need since their ultimate aim is to determine how school outcomes can be improved. Even for those schools considered exemplary, assessing programs has the potential for taking student performance to still higher levels.

The previous paragraphs opened this book when the first edition was published in 2003. Since then, the pressures educators face to raise student achievement still continue. In responding to this effort, many recent books and journal articles written from classroom and leadership perspectives have added to the literature by providing worthwhile advice to improve student outcomes. You are now looking at another work that seeks to do the same thing. What contribution can it make to help practitioners do what is expected of them? I would like to answer by stating that this book is designed to serve as a practical reference for school personnel to conduct their own assessments of the curriculums they have in place. Why should they want to do this? Because when a school makes provision for regularly performing program evaluations, it puts into place a mechanism for monitoring the extent to which its curriculums contribute to student success. In this regard, evaluation of a program helps determine whether to expend the time or effort to make changes in it or seek another one with greater potential.

Why not just examine standardized test results and implement needed remedial strategies accordingly? The answer to this is that such an approach cannot do what a sound program assessment can. First of all, test scores should not be considered the only indicator of school performance, and as discussed later in the book, there should be others as well. With regard to the *process* involved in evaluating a program, this endeavor determines in a more in-depth and comprehensive way factors that enhance or hinder effective delivery of instruction. Thus program evaluation involves obtaining perspectives from different groups—faculty, the administrator(s), students, and parents. Their input leads to greater understanding of the various aspects of how a program functions and its outcomes. Having the benefit of these insights puts the school in a stronger position to meet expectations held for it by the community and its district.

Engaging in program evaluation by the very people responsible for producing results has the effect of strengthening the operation of a school because its personnel are involved firsthand in planning and implementing data-driven actions to increase student achievement. In this regard, when individuals collaborate in a project designed to help them do their job better, they are more apt to relate to and accept the recommendations for improvement because they are part of the solution. This is a productive position to be in; it changes how people regard and respond to situations. Thus teachers become proactive participants in change initiatives, rather than reacting to the results yielded by high-stakes testing.

According to the results of mandated testing, a school may not do as well as it would have liked. However, the fact that it set up the machinery for assessing the effectiveness of a program is in and of itself a worthwhile endeavor because faculty would be able to guide future efforts based on what they have learned from an evaluation. Moreover, providing for self-corrective actions communicates to the public that the school has taken another step to improve its work.

For practitioners themselves, taking an active role toward making a situation better can contribute to people feeling that they are more in control and are thereby more optimistic about how change will turn out. It should be pointed out, however, that as discussed in this book, program evaluation is not all about finding where modifications should be made in a curriculum. It is just as important to confirm the extent to which a program is finding success in accomplishing its goals. Both perspectives have implications for enhancing organizational performance since program evaluation carried out regularly in a school has a systemic effect. In this regard, it discloses information that can be useful for linking the efforts of teachers across grade levels or within departments.

Given this background, program evaluation can help bypass, or at least ease the frustration, of seeing one's hard and sincere efforts directed at helping students learn but not meet standards. From this perspective, teaching those with different levels of attitude and motivation is difficult enough without having the benefits of a well-designed program. Under these circumstances, a teacher has to improvise and rely on his or her own ingenuity to think of instructional strategies and learning activities to prepare students for the realities of mandated testing. Beyond satisfying this need, as educators well know, teaching in and of itself can be a joyful experience because as the beginning of this introduction indicates, it can help make students be and feel successful. When they are, teachers who were instrumental in contributing to this outcome will consequently feel that they have been successful as well. This feeling is a defining characteristic of what it means to win. It connotes a sense of having accomplished something worthwhile and a promise of further progress to be made for both teachers and students.[1]

In the context of winning, effective teaching and an excellent program makes for an unbeatable combination. It finds expression in students becoming more engaged in the learning process, mastering material challenging to them at their ability level, and ultimately, achieving higher—the underlying theme of this book.

ABOUT THIS EDITION

As with my earlier work,[2] I wanted this version to be one that could be used by practitioners themselves in their local building, hence the term *site-based program evaluation*, an underlying theme of this book. This perspective was taken because programs should be assessed in the context of where they are delivered. To this end, there are substantive changes in the current edition that I believe would facilitate carrying out on-site projects. The following are highlights:

There is greater reliance on the use of percentages. Since educators are used to working with these, this makes it easier to analyze data. Additional figures have been included. These serve to synthesize the procedures involved in carrying out the phases of an evaluation as described in Chapters 7 and 8. The use of graphs to display the results of an evaluation is new to this edition. In Chapter 4, a formative evaluation approach has been added to determine if and how improvements should be made to a modified program being tested experimentally. More items have been included in the needs assessment. A miniguide for the evaluation team leader has been added. Finally, more detailed explanations and examples have been incorporated in various chapters to clarify the assessment process.

PURPOSE OF THE BOOK

Guidelines are provided that a team of faculty members can apply to evaluate ongoing programs that are either a regular or an ancillary part of the curriculum. Moreover, the techniques presented can also be used to evaluate programs recently completed.

The focus is on analyzing program processes and student performance. The latter can include academic or vocational outcomes, or can concern development in other areas, such as improving self-concept or discipline. Investigating the processes used to deliver the program is essential since they determine in large measure the curriculum's impact as well as the attitudes of students and faculty toward its instructional activities. In this regard, evaluation of processes identifies specific factors operating at the core of the program that may be inhibiting successful outcomes. Such disclosure aids in generating solutions that could lead to improved student achievement. For this purpose, the methodology for obtaining, analyzing, and using "process" information is covered.

ORGANIZATION OF THE BOOK

This book is designed for practitioners with little or no experience in evaluating programs. Thus this activity offers an opportunity for further professional development.

The contents are organized so that Chapters 1–6 build a foundation of knowledge and attitudes applicable to conducting an evaluation study. Numerous examples are provided in order to clarify the various tasks involved in this process. Chapters 7–10 take the reader through the steps of the evaluation process, while Chapter 11 highlights the importance of the principal's leadership in program evaluation. More specifically, the following are covered.

Chapter 1 reviews various perspectives on program evaluation, with a view toward school improvement. In this regard, the benefits of site-based evaluation are identified, and the cyclical process of formative and summative methodology is also described.

The theme of Chapter 2 is essentially that program evaluation is a natural feature of a learning organization since it provides a mechanism for gaining insights about which aspects of the curriculum produced the best learning conditions and which need to be strengthened. Characteristic of a learning organization, a systems approach to increase student achievement is also treated.

Chapter 3 describes how evaluation carried out to improve student achievement strengthens the link that connects assessment results, a curriculum's ongoing development, and progressively higher student performance. Background for conducting experiments as an outgrowth of assessing a program is provided. In the next chapter guidelines are given for various experimental approaches to determine if modifications based on assessing a curriculum are effective.

Chapter 5 covers various perspectives on the role of collaboration in carrying out a program evaluation. Included are the advantages of having a faculty evaluation team, steps the principal can take in forming one as well as recommendations for the team leader to help the group do its work effectively and efficiently. How the team can collaborate with the staff members whose program is being evaluated is also featured.

Chapter 6 discusses the types of data—quantitative and qualitative—to use in measuring outcomes of a program evaluation, validity, and reliability of evaluation data, and how the evaluation team would communicate practical techniques to the faculty to determine test validity and reliability.

Chapters 7 and 8 describe the steps involved in carrying out Phases 1 through 3 and 4 through 6 of the evaluation process. This involves the use of a specific set of questions to guide the evaluation and how data can be analyzed by approaches that are readily applied by practitioners.

In Chapter 9, the contents of an evaluation report are described along with a checklist to track its completion. How the evaluation project can be assessed from two perspectives—formative and summative—is discussed in Chapter 10. Chapter 11 revisits the role of the principal with respect to helping to ensure that the evaluation project is a success. Finally, as indicated previously, a miniguide for the evaluation team leader has been added as an Appendix to this edition. It is in the form of a checklist encompassing the major tasks of an evaluation project.

Guidelines are presented that encompass actions leaders can take to help ensure that program evaluation as a tool for organization development has an opportunity to accomplish its purpose of providing direction for improving school outcomes. Therefore, how the leadership roles of the administration and faculty can be integrated synergistically with program evaluation and reflective practice to enhance the effectiveness and efficiency of a learning organization is also discussed.

Note that a distinction has been made between effectiveness and efficiency as criteria of organizational functioning. Effectiveness refers to the extent to which goals have been accomplished, whereas efficiency considers the extent to which resources, financial and human, have been expended in accomplishing goals.

THRIVING IN AN ENVIRONMENT OF HIGH-STAKES ASSESSMENT

Decisions based on test results that may substantially or even adversely affect students as well as administrators and teachers characterize high-stakes assessment (Jenkins, 1993). Despite the many critics who disparage the use of standardized tests to determine if schools are successful, these tests, at least in the foreseeable future, are not going to be discontinued.[3] One reason for this is that their results provide a uniform and relatively easily understood means of communicating to different groups the performance of a single student, a class, a school, or a district. Furthermore, findings from standardized testing provide a clear target to aim for when administrators and faculty seek improvement.

It is not the intent at this point to argue the benefits and limitations of standardized tests. In the final analysis, they constitute the reality that teachers and leaders at the building or district levels must deal with in this era of accountability. This should not be construed as negative. Helping students do well on these tests can serve as a challenge, a word not being used lightly here. Human experience teaches us that when individuals and groups confront difficult situations, they call on inner, untapped resources that enable them to meet these situations and grow stronger as a result. This means that educators who see only the downside of high-stakes assessment should instead regard standardized testing as an opportunity for growth.

The willingness of school personnel to assess their own work is an indicator of professionalism that can be expressed through program evaluation projects. In this regard, this book offers an approach to results-oriented inquiry that should pass the crucible of practicality.

A CONCLUDING NOTE

The importance of the leader's role in program evaluation is reiterated at various points in this book. With this orientation, the work describes the methodology to conduct a creditable evaluation. However, the principal needs to communicate to the staff that program evaluation is an integral part of the organizational fabric and follow up with leadership behaviors to actualize this priority. Otherwise, program evaluation projects are destined to become another school reform technique added to the heap of "tried but didn't work" initiatives. Thus the call to leadership is heightened so that this situation is not likely to occur.

NOTES

1. Along these lines, Sommers (1995) refers to a sense of accomplishment when people feel they have completed "something to which . . . [they have] dedicated a lot of effort" (p. 13).

2. The previous edition of this book is the outgrowth of a paper presented at the first Phi Delta Kappa International Conference on Effective Schools in 1999. The presentation involved a modification of materials the author has used with his graduate courses concerning program evaluation.

3. That No Child Left Behind standards must be met by 2014 supports the point of continued use of standardized test results.

Acknowledgments

I would like to thank the following individuals who have helped me in various ways in writing this book:

Cathy Hernandez, Acquisitions Editor at Corwin Press, for her support, interest in my work, and positive comments about the book's potential. Your confidence in advocating a second edition is most gratifying, and I appreciate your efforts on my behalf.

Belinda Thresher, Director of Production at Appingo, who helped get the book ready for publication. Your cooperation in planning, the useful information you provided, and responsiveness to the various questions I raised during the course of the project facilitated completing my work.

The staff at Corwin Press and Appingo, for the efforts expended in the production of this book as well as the reviewers for their useful feedback.

Dr. Cozette Buckney, for taking time from your busy schedule to write the foreword for this book as you did for the first edition when you were Chief of Staff for the Chicago Public Schools. In acknowledging your contribution to the first edition I indicated that, "since this work is designed primarily for practitioners, it is indeed gratifying to have an endorsement from a person who has occupied important leadership roles in the field." This sentiment is the same today as before. Your work with the Philadelphia and St. Louis schools and now with the New Orleans School District speaks to your continued dedication to education. I am honored by your willingness to again write the foreword. Your reputation and professionalism, being so widely recognized, makes your endorsement one that I greatly appreciate.

Dr. Andy Henrikson and Dr. Dennis Pauli, for their useful feedback. Their comments from the perspective of experienced school administrators is much appreciated.

Martin Cohn, J.D., Attorney at Law, who has always expressed interest in my work. In the first edition I indicated that I was very fortunate, indeed, to have known you for so long, and to have experienced your sharp wit, wise council, and keen insights. Today these words still hold true, including your especially valued friendship. I wish to thank you for your continued support and encouragement that has extended to this second edition.

PUBLISHER'S ACKNOWLEDGMENTS

Corwin Press gratefully acknowledges the contributions of the following reviewers:

Judy Brunner, Principal
Parkview High School, Springfield, MO

Henry Frierson, Professor of Measurement and Evaluation
University of North Carolina, Chapel Hill, NC

Arlen R. Gullickson, Director of the Evaluation Center
Western Michigan University, Kalamazoo, MI

Katherine Hayes, Chief Education Research Scientist
Program Evaluation and Research Branch
Los Angeles Unified School District, CA

Cheri Hodson, Educational Research Analyst
Program Evaluation and Research Branch
Los Angeles Unified School District, CA

Debbie Johnson, Principal
Lunt School, Falmouth, ME

Roger Kaufman, Professor of Educational Psychology and
    Learning Systems
Florida State University, Tallahassee, FL

Marie Kraska, Professor of Educational Foundations,
    Leadership, and Technology
Auburn University, AL

Rebecca A. Maynard, Professor of Education and Social Policy
University of Pennsylvania, PA

Todd Twyman, Assistant Professor of Behavioral Research,
    Teaching, and Educational Leadership
University of Oregon, Eugene, OR

About the Author

Martin H. Jason is Professor of Educational Leadership at Roosevelt University in Chicago where he has served as Director of the Educational Administration and Supervision Program, and is currently Director of the Ed.D. Program in Educational Leadership. He teaches courses in leadership, quantitative research methods, and program evaluation, and has over forty years of university teaching experience. His doctorate in educational administration and supervision was earned at the University of Illinois at Urbana.

Dr. Jason has presented many papers concerning leadership at national and regional conferences. His articles have appeared in *Planning and Changing*, the *High School Journal*, and *Research for Educational Reform*. He has also written a chapter for the book *Creating High Functioning Schools*.

1

Perspectives on Program Evaluation

No matter the area—academics, sports, music, or any other endeavor—in order to improve performance, current efforts *must* be evaluated. In this regard, program evaluation is indispensable for school improvement. Given this position, this chapter presents a case for local schools to conduct their own program evaluations, with a view toward raising student achievement. Also covered are the goals of program evaluation, how formative and summative evaluation methods complement each other, and the role of evaluation in program development.

HOW PROGRAM EVALUATION CONTRIBUTES TO SCHOOL IMPROVEMENT

Evaluation provides a tool for determining the extent to which a program[1] or curriculum is effective and, at the same time, indicates direction for remediating processes of the curriculum that do not contribute to successful student performance. Thus program evaluation serves two organizational functions—it confirms and it diagnoses (see Figure 1.1).

Figure 1.1   The Functions of Program Evaluation

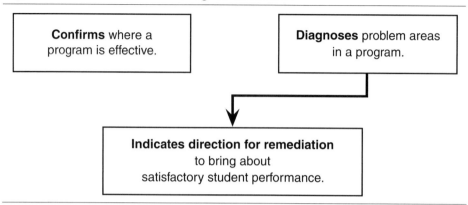

Information disclosed by these functions enhances organizational efficiency by providing a focus for faculty and administrator efforts. This allows resources, in terms of time and money, to be directed at the areas of greatest need. As indicated in Figure 1.2, concentrating efforts where they are most needed helps ensure higher achievement levels. World-class athletes and superstars in the performing arts know this instinctively and work relentlessly to improve those aspects of their performance they know detract from their achieving an even higher level of excellence.

Educators can and should follow the example of superstars in other arenas. Delivering instructional activities is a performing art (Hasenstab & Wilson, 1989) albeit one grounded in a science of pedagogical principles and concepts.

Figure 1.2   How Progam Evaluation Contributes to School Improvement

- Evaluation is a tool for determining effectiveness of a program or curriculum (confirms).
- Evaluation results indicate direction for remediating unsuccessful processes of the curriculum (diagnoses).
- Evaluation enhances organizational efficiency by providing a focus for faculty and administrator efforts.
- Enhanced organizational efficiency allows resources (time and money) to be directed at the areas of greatest need.

Principal and Faculty Leadership in Program Evaluation

For the principal and other school leaders who orchestrate the planning and implementing of programs and for faculty who carry out learning activities, improving student performance is linked to improvement in processes that influence the effectiveness of teaching and learning. This approach is facilitated when the organizational structure of the school includes an evaluation team[2] that conducts program assessments on an ongoing basis.[3]

Against this background, program evaluation carried out by practitioners holds great promise for improving student achievement as reflected by test scores and other indicators. However, no evaluation project can reach its potential effectiveness without the leadership of the principal in promoting, supporting, and facilitating the assessment process. At the same time, no principal should take on the responsibility of managing an evaluation project. Doing so would take too much time from performing other administrative tasks, inhibit the professional development of staff members, and minimize or even eliminate the feeling of their ownership in the endeavor. Consequently, the satisfaction that accompanies the belief that one is part of some worthwhile activity would be lessened. When the faculty has positive attitudes about their work, they produce self-sustaining energy because their efforts are likely to be gratifying, rather than being perceived as onerous.

Since the principal should not manage an evaluation project, there is a definite need for authentic faculty leadership to take the initiatives required for conducting an evaluation study as well as for carrying out the monitoring and follow-up of activities to ensure its success. To this end, the role of the leader of an evaluation team, along with the responsibilities of its members, are described in Chapter 5.

BENEFITS OF SITE-BASED PROGRAM EVALUATION

Why should practitioners in a local school assess their own programs?[4] This is a valid question given the pressures, time constraints, and stress faced by busy and often harried educators whose scrutiny of their work by the public, media, and legislators has translated into increasing demands for accountability. Criticism of schools for their culpability regarding substandard test performance has become a constant drone that is enervating for administrators and faculty alike.

In an environment where educators find themselves feeling defensive about their efforts and consequently working harder to meet and stave off further criticism, local school personnel are unlikely to relish taking on the additional responsibility of evaluating programs. This is understandable considering all they have to do to meet higher level expectations.

Given this situation, is conducting a systematic, ongoing program evaluation worth the time and effort? It definitely is, since this process functions as an organization development tool that can enhance professional growth and, correspondingly, student performance. Both goals would be accomplished because inherent in assessment projects is a guidance mechanism to facilitate identifying those aspects of the program's operation that may need modification. When these are in place, teachers are likely to find that with a more effective program, less time will have to be spent on reteaching those students who initially had difficulty grasping the material. Thus evaluation of a program can make delivering it more efficient. Moreover, by conducting their own evaluation of the extent to which a program impacts student performance, educators demonstrate a willingness to be accountable to the outside community.[5] Figure 1.3 summarizes major advantages of each school assessing its own programs.

Figure 1.3   Benefits of Site-Based Program Evaluation

- Evaluation enhances professional growth.
- Evaluation results identify program weaknesses and lead to improvement.
- Improved programs enhance student performance.
- Educators involved in evaluation demonstrate a willingness to be accountable to the outside community.

GOALS OF PROGRAM EVALUATION

Several aspects of program evaluation are germane to the scope of this book. The following captures the intent of the content covered. For Brainard (1996),

> effective program evaluation is a systematic process that focuses on program improvement and renewal and on discovering peaks of program excellence. Program evaluation should be viewed as an important ongoing activity, one that goes beyond research or simple fact-finding to inform decisions about the future shape of the program under study. (p. 5)

In this vein,

> program evaluation contributes to quality services by providing feedback from program activities and outcomes to those who can make changes in programs or who decide which services are to be offered. Without feedback, human service programs (indeed, any activity) cannot be carried out effectively. (Posavac & Carey, 2007, p. 14)

According to M. L. Smith and Glass (1987), based on evidence, value judgments are applied to determine a program's effectiveness. DeRoche (1987) provides a set of "principles of evaluation" relevant to the practitioner orientation of this book. Among them, he maintains that the evaluation process should

- promote a positive attitude toward self-appraisal and self-improvement;
- provide opportunities for school personnel to diagnose difficulties;
- strengthen existing programs and establish pilot programs or projects to test new approaches;
- help teachers and learners determine the extent to which each has been successful in the teaching-learning process; and

- encourage a team effort, a cooperative spirit, and a feeling by the community that all are accountable for the education of our young people (p. 9).

Against the background of these authors' perspectives, conducting a site-based evaluation study fits within the scope of reflective practice. In this regard, an evaluation project offers a stimulus for administrators and staff to deliberate about their efforts and base subsequent actions on what they have analyzed.

TWO EVALUATION METHODS

Based on the work of Scriven, who in 1967 differentiated between two evaluation approaches—formative and summative—Fitzpatrick, Sanders, and Worthen (2004) describe these methods. They indicate that formative evaluation provides useful information for improving a program. In contrast, through summative evaluation, judgments are made about a "program's worth or merit in relation to important criteria" (p. 17).

Consistent with the guidelines presented in this book, Fitzpatrick et al. (2004) refer to a 1991 work by Scriven in which they indicated that "the results of [a] study may be used for both summative, and, later, formative evaluation purposes" (p. 19).

ASSESSING PROGRAM PROCESSES

While a summative evaluation will determine the extent to which a program has been successful, the key to improving school outcomes lies in analyzing how the program operates and in making any needed adjustments. The reason for this is that the quality of the activities (processes) used to carry out a program can affect its outcomes (Weiss, 1998). Thus summative evaluation can only go so far in suggesting areas of improvement since the information it provides is used to "summarize" evidence concerning the impact of the program. Whereas with formative evaluation, more specific ways to refine the processes (including materials) for delivering the curriculum are suggested. Put another way, summative evaluation provides a "barometer" by which indicators are measured to gauge how effectively a program has accomplished (or is accomplishing) its goals. But what also needs to be studied are the processes used in implementing instructional activities of the program.[6]

Formative Evaluation

As covered in Chapter 7, there are also factors (e.g., teacher collaboration and students' preparedness for learning current content) that can affect instructional activities and can apply to any curriculum. Both curriculum processes and related factors provide the dynamics that determine the degree to which a program is functional. Studying these dynamics falls within the scope of formative evaluation since this type of assessment could disclose information leading to program improvement. Thus analyzing formative information provides the "how-to" dimension of program evaluation because, as described later in this book, opinions are elicited primarily from program staff on actions to take to improve the processes and factors related to the delivery of a curriculum. Such opinions, while subjective, rely on evidence of student achievement and reactions linked to activities of the program.

In performance terms, formative evaluation provides the focus needed to concentrate on remediating those areas where less than optimum conditions inhibit higher levels of overall student proficiency. Therefore, formative evaluation contributes data to enable a program to be strengthened by guiding decisions on the direction(s) a program should take (Fitzpatrick et al., 2004). These decisions are guided by the feedback mechanism that becomes engaged with a formative orientation as may be noted in the works of such writers as DeRoche (1987), Fitzpatrick et al. (2004), Posavac and Carey (2007), and Weiss (1998).

Formative evaluation, according to Fitzpatrick et al. (2004), is useful when a program's development is in its early stages. Thus before a program has been carried out too long, it can be improved by formative assessment. However, since outcomes depend on the processes used to

Figure 1.4 Complementary Approaches to Program Evaluation

	Formative	**Summative**
Purpose:	To improve a program's operation by examining its processes	To judge the worth, merit, or success of a program based on its effectiveness in meeting goals
When conducted:	In the early stages of a program's implementation and at the time a summative assessment is made	At the end of a program or agreed upon date after it has been in operation for a sufficient length of time to measure its impact
Data source:	Relies primarily on opinions from staff delivering the program on how it can be improved	Student outcomes (e.g., test and attitude scores); opinions of students, teachers, administrators, and parents

achieve them, in keeping with the recommendation of these authors, a formative evaluation approach should be integrated with a summative study. Figure 1.4 highlights the compatibility of both assessment methods.[7]

While not diminishing the importance of summative evaluation, assessment of school programs should place heavy emphasis on formative methodology.[8] This perspective is in keeping with a defining characteristic of effective leaders in that they continually seek to improve problematic situations. Driving this outlook is their discontent with the status quo.[9] A corollary of this disposition is a leader's conviction communicated to the staff that "we can change what we need to." This belief has implications for professional development of the faculty and correspondingly enhances efforts in helping students reach their potential. However, no matter how well this belief is conveyed, and even if it galvanizes a staff to work toward agreed-upon common goals, the enthusiasm for these will become short-lived without the mechanism for their attainment. In this regard, personnel in an individual school who are well versed in program evaluation methodology will be in a more knowledgeable and empowering position to effect change. Both formative and summative evaluation methods are related when efforts are directed toward program improvement as reflected in the following discussion.

LINKING EVALUATION WITH PROGRAM IMPROVEMENT

The process of improving a curriculum as described in this book is cyclical.[10] From this perspective, a current program is evaluated with respect to its outcomes (summative) and the processes that produced them (formative). Changes designed to improve instructional activities that are feasible to implement are incorporated into a revised program. Next, the modified curriculum is tested experimentally and then reassessed summatively and formatively at an agreed-upon later date (e.g., toward the end of the school year).

Applying these evaluation methods provides direction for improving the program. Thus program development is iterative. Each cycle leads to higher levels of curriculum quality, continually evolving in its content and delivery as program staff learn from their efforts. Figure 1.5 illustrates the program improvement cycle.

The entire process is grounded in a systems approach to organizational improvement. In this regard, the modified program is also referred to as an intervention since it represents a new factor introduced into the individual school as an open system.

The concept and dynamics of a systems approach to organizational performance is treated in Chapter 2. At this point, however, it should be mentioned that an intervention also represents an innovative program since some of its features would be newly added. Finally, if it is decided

Figure 1.5   Cyclical Process of Improving Curriculum

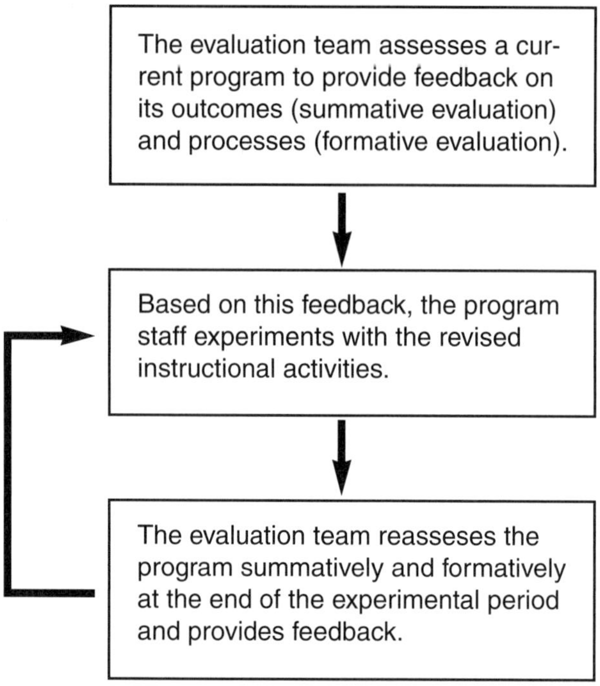

The evaluation team assesses a current program to provide feedback on its outcomes (summative evaluation) and processes (formative evaluation).

Based on this feedback, the program staff experiments with the revised instructional activities.

The evaluation team reasseses the program summatively and formatively at the end of the experimental period and provides feedback.

that, based on an evaluation, a program ought to be discontinued and replaced with a more promising alternative, then this action can also be considered program development. The rationale for this is that the change represents the evolution of what may be a better curricular offering.

A CONCLUDING NOTE

The assessment approach taken in this book considers a program or a curriculum as a "work in progress" because those who deliver it should constantly seek to improve how its instructional activities are carried out, realizing that there could always be ways to make the process more effective and efficient. The notion of something being "in progress" does not imply that a lower standard is maintained until the program is finalized as a polished package, ready to be taught. No curriculum should be considered as ultimate.[11]

The price for excellence and beyond is continued effort. This is a good price to pay. This metaphor should be conveyed by leaders to their staff and, in turn, faculty should communicate it to their students because we do not know—and can never know—what can be finally achieved. To have such knowledge is a logical impossibility since the more we learn, the more our capacity to grow increases.

From an existential perspective, our existence as educators and the existence of those whose lives we touch in our roles can be immeasurably enhanced by unleashing the growth tendencies inherent in all human beings. "Unleashing" is an apt connotation because, under the right circumstances, limits to one's learning become unfettered. Too idealistic? Too unrealistic? No! What is unrealistic are situations that prevent us from being who we really are and really can be.

Could a curriculum produce substantial change in students, not only from a knowledge perspective, but also in a way that promotes their creativity? Without doubt it can, if the program is effective and efficient in accomplishing these goals. Thus when meaningful learning activities are added to the equation, the dynamic for student and faculty growth is engaged.

In this vein, if the curriculum can be systematic in its plan and execution, and if program evaluation can be conducted systematically, then the confluence of both approaches should enable the continuous improvement of teaching and learning.

CHAPTER 1 HIGHLIGHTS

1. Program evaluation is indispensable for school improvement. It confirms the extent to which a program or curriculum is effective and, at the same time, indicates direction for remediating processes of the curriculum that do not contribute to successful student performance.

2. No evaluation project can reach its potential without the leadership of the principal. However, a principal should not manage the project. There is a definite need for authentic faculty leadership to take the initiatives required for conducting an evaluation study as well as carrying out the monitoring and follow-up activities to ensure the project's success.

3. Conducting systematic, ongoing program evaluation is worth the time and effort since this process functions as an organization development tool that can enhance professional growth and, correspondingly, student performance.

4. By conducting their own evaluation of the extent to which a program impacts student achievement, evaluators demonstrate a willingness to be accountable to the outside community.

5. Summative evaluation determines the extent to which a program has accomplished or is accomplishing its goals. Formative evaluation provides information for improving the implementation of a program. The latter approach should be integrated into a summative study.

6. Evaluation of school programs should place heavy emphasis on formative methodology. This perspective is in keeping with a defining characteristic of effective leaders in that they continually seek to improve problematic situations.

7.   Personnel in an individual school who are well versed in program evaluation methodology will be in a more knowledgeable and empowering position to effect change.

8.   If the curriculum can be systematically planned and executed, and if program evaluation can also be conducted systematically, then the confluence of both approaches should enable the continuous improvement of instruction.

9.   The process of improving a curriculum is cyclical. As such, a current program is analyzed with respect to its outcomes and the processes that produced them. Next, modifications are made that are designed to enhance instructional activities. The modified curriculum is then tested experimentally and reassessed summatively at a later date.

NOTES

1. Program is a broad term that includes, but is not limited to, curricula (Gredler, 1996).

2. DeRoche (1987) refers to an evaluation committee rather than an evaluation team. Its function encompasses evaluating programs and other areas (e.g., faculty meetings and teacher effectiveness).

3. That program evaluation should be ongoing is consistent with what Brainard (1996) and DeRoche (1987) advocate.

4. Carrying out site-based evaluations is in keeping with one of the trends of program evaluation identified by Fitzpatrick et al. (2004). This often involves empowering "stakeholders to conduct their own evaluations" (p. 44).

5. The use of evaluation to determine accountability is also cited in the literature (e.g., DeRoche, 1987; Joint Committee on Standards for Educational Evaluation, 1994; Posavac & Carey, 2007; Weiss, 1998).

6. According to Weiss (1998), how well a program teaches is one example of the processes that should be assessed by evaluators.

7. Other perspectives on the differences between formative and summative evaluation are also presented in figure form by Fitzpatrick et al. (2004).

8. DeRoche (1987) favors formative as compared to summative evaluation. He points out that principals and teachers can make changes based on formative feedback during a program or project rather than waiting for its completion.

9. In discussing the school improvement process, DuFour and Eaker (1992) call attention to how innovation is blocked by accepting the status quo.

10. DeRoche (1987) presents a ten-step curriculum improvement cycle that he relates to the evaluation process.

11. Weiss (1998) regards many programs as never finished since they continually change, not always due to improved strategies. However, she maintains that most often evaluation involves formative information to help staff improve their programs.

2

How Program Evaluation Contributes to a Learning Organization

This chapter describes the spirit that pervades the school as a learning organization. The connection of such an organization with program evaluation and reflective practice is also discussed. How the parts of the school organization can be linked by leadership attitudes and actions that promote viewing the school as a system is treated. From this perspective, various roles and functions of the school are viewed as interdependent, which thereby facilitates efforts directed at improving student achievement.

THE SPIRIT OF A LEARNING ORGANIZATION

Conducting a sound program evaluation extends beyond technique. It is part of an overriding mentality that those who aspire to higher levels of performance can readily embrace—the unremitting pursuit of excellence. This drive is captured in "*kaizen*, a Japanese word that connotes an ongoing spirit of concern with incremental but relentless improvement, however small" (Schmoker, 1999, p. 51). Based on McTighe's position advocating that schools adopt a spirit of kaizen, Schmoker argues that this spirit, with its emphasis on steady improvement, provides the power to combat fatalism in schools. He maintains that this can be achieved through, for example, feedback obtained from quarterly assessments, which indicates that "we are moving forward and becoming more capable" (Schmoker, 1999, p. 52). Drawing on the work of Wiggins, Schmoker also points out that small improvements should not be overlooked because to do so could affect teacher morale.

Adopting this spirit of kaizen does not necessarily limit us to small increments of growth. While it is essential for principals to recognize noticeable student and faculty accomplishments, principals should also use indicators of improvement as springboards to create a vision of even higher possibilities. Thus great things can be achieved when there is great vision. The words of Chicago architect Daniel Burnham reflect this poignantly: "Make no little plans; they have no magic to stir men's blood."

The anticipation of what students and faculty can accomplish can be realized when the curriculum is designed to optimize learning. Underlying this goal is the spirit of kaizen—a belief and feeling that pervades the individual school as an institution that is continually evolving because its members relate to the logical connection between their own growth and that of the school. This is the essence of the learning organization.

THE SCHOOL AS A LEARNING ORGANIZATION

Senge (1990) defines a learning organization as one "that is continually expanding its capacity to create its future" (p. 14). In terms of performance, he maintains that organizations that will truly excel will be those that have discovered "how to tap people's commitment and capacity to learn at all levels in an organization" (p. 4).

The notion that learning is evident at all levels in organizations that excel is philosophically compatible with the transformational leadership model. This may be noted from Burns's (1978) concept of transforming leadership.[1] He maintains that leaders and followers are both transformed because they are engaged in ways that mutually raise their motivation and morality and, consequently, their conduct and ethical aspirations.

Given the characteristics of a learning organization and transformational leadership, administrators who are open to their own potential for growth are likely to promote an environment that motivates and facilitates staff development. Moreover, collaboration between the principal and faculty to design a meaningful curriculum is, indeed, an ethical endeavor. Thus the choice of learning activities, by definition, affects the quality of school life for students as well as faculty. These activities should be perceived as worthwhile and desirable goals, since how individuals are required to spend time can elevate or lower the value of their experiences and, consequently, their feelings toward the organization.

Program evaluation regularly carried out is a natural feature of a school as a learning organization. As such, its members can gain insights about which aspects of the curriculum produced the best learning conditions and which aspects need to be strengthened. Along these lines, Posavac and Carey (2007) recommend that a learning culture be encouraged in which evaluation findings are effectively used. Accordingly, they maintain that in this way, program directors and staff would not hide from failure but instead learn from experiments.

The connection between this attitude and transformational leadership may be noted from a 1993 report of research conducted by Leithwood, Dart, Jantzi, and Steinbach (as cited in Leithwood, 1994). They found that one of the behaviors characteristic of principals displaying transformational leadership was their removal of penalties for making mistakes in professional and school improvement efforts. Consistent with the thrust of self-assessment of programs, these administrators also encouraged "staff to evaluate their practices and refine them as needed" (Leithwood, 1994, p. 511).

Another behavior of the principal associated with the transformational leadership model developed by Leithwood (with various colleagues), involves having the staff "think reflectively and critically about their own practices" (Leithwood, Leonard, & Sharratt, 1998, p. 249).

REFLECTIVE PRACTICE

Guiding the various phases of an evaluation project—from planning its design, to collecting and analyzing data, drawing conclusions, and offering recommendations for improvement—requires systematic thought, both individual and collective (see Figure 2.1). In this vein, reflective practice is integral for assessing programs as suggested by the following definition based primarily on the work of Monti et al. (1998). Reflective practice is a cognitive process engaged in by one or more persons confronted by a problem situation that involves evaluation of values, goals, beliefs, policies, and practices, with a view toward implementing actions to improve the quality of school life for students and school personnel.

Figure 2.1 Phases of an Evaluation Project

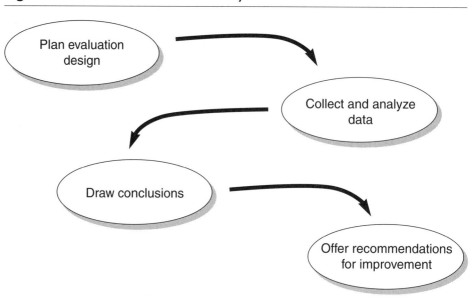

Given this definition, reflective practice is inherent in a learning organization. It serves as an overriding dynamic for personnel and institutional growth because progress depends on how we think about situations and, accordingly, how we act based on our conceptions.

Fundamentally, there are two dimensions to reflective thought—attitude and competency. In this vein, Senge (1990) introduces the concept of reflective openness and holds that it involves a "willingness to challenge our own thinking" (p. 277) as well as certain skills such as team learning through dialogue and discussion.

Since engaging in reflective practice involves examining problem situations, the connection between this activity and the disposition of a learning organization may be noted from Leithwood et al. (1998). They point out that the stimulus for organizational learning "is assumed to be prompted by some felt need . . . or perception of a problem prompted from inside or outside the school that leads to a collective search for a solution" (p. 248). This search is facilitated through a program evaluation project since its activities are oriented systematically and comprehensively toward addressing a problem. In this context, problems are indispensable for personal and professional growth because their solutions often require creative approaches that can constitute curriculum modifications, which in turn increase student motivation and learning.[2]

Thus perceptions become our reality. From a phenomenological perspective, "all behavior is a function of the individual's perceptions" (Combs & Snygg, 1959, p. 18). Put another way, to paraphrase Shakespeare, nothing is bad, but thinking makes it so. The practical implications of this axiom are profound: regard a problem as difficult, and it becomes so; regard a problem as an opportunity for improvement, and it becomes so. There is nothing unique about this statement—its message abounds in motivational literature.

That "problems should be considered opportunities" is not a trite maxim. It is embedded in the mentality of a learning organization and is indispensable for systemic change. In this regard, promoting the attitude of determination and faith that improvements can and will be made, coupled with the confidence that we have the collective abilities to bring this about, provides a potent synergy that ripples throughout the school organization felt by staff and students alike.

Athletes and their coaches know well the potency of positive attitudes. It is the major factor that sustains them when fatigue sets in and, moreover, counteracts doubts and discouragement. Attitude also divides; it can differentiate world-class stars in any sport or performing art by the edge it gives the winner. In short, communicating a positive outlook toward school improvement efforts—from the initiative through implementation stages—is the ultimate leadership strategy. With a positive attitude, interventions are more likely to succeed. In contrast, a corollary of a negative attitude is lower expectations, and correspondingly, lower performance—grist for the frustration mill.

While a positive attitude motivates and sustains, it can only go so far. Thus attitudes without corresponding actions are short lived (see Figure 2.2). This situation can lead to cynicism on the part of the faculty who may come to believe that expressions of positive attitudes are just slogans, rhetoric, or exhortations that leaders are supposed to spout.

Figure 2.2   The Power of Attitude on Action

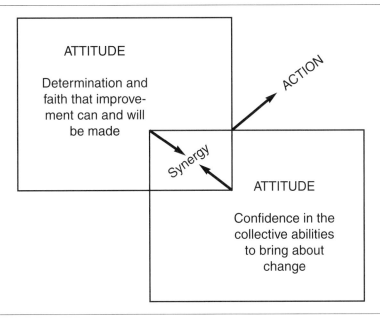

A structure for taking appropriate actions by the school as a learning organization is the evaluation team. The work of the team is greatly enhanced when the members of the organization at all levels adopt a systems mentality. This perspective is an overriding aspect of the learning organization as conceptualized by Senge (1990).

LINKING THE PARTS OF THE SCHOOL ORGANIZATION FOR IMPROVED PERFORMANCE

According to Senge (1990), "systems thinking is a discipline for seeing wholes. It is a framework for seeing interrelationships rather than things, for seeing patterns of change rather than 'snapshots'" (p. 68). For Senge, relying on snapshots means focusing on isolated parts of the system, with the result that the "deepest problems never seem to get solved" (p. 7). This malady can be prevented if we engage in systems thinking since Senge maintains that such thinking involves "leverage—seeing where actions and changes in structures can lead to significant, enduring improvements" (p. 114). Moreover, according to Senge, leverage also encompasses the notion that "small, well-focused actions can sometimes produce significant enduring improvements if they're in the right place" (p. 64).

When individuals engage in systems thinking, they can better understand the interconnectiveness of their work in the school organization. This insight facilitates higher organizational performance by bringing collective wisdom, produced through reflective practice, to bear on problems that prevent curricular processes from functioning optimally, thereby restricting student outcomes.

While theoretically systems thinking may be potentially effective and efficient, the physical arrangement of schools, with their compartmentalized classroom structure,[3] is not designed to promote this perspective. In this regard, Schmoker (1999) cites Lortie's 1975 classic book *Schoolteacher* when referring to the negative aspects of teachers' isolationism and individualism inherent in their work. This situation "thwarts . . . [teachers] from developing common solutions through dialogue. Isolation tacitly assumes that practitioners have nothing to learn from each other" (Schmoker, 1999, p. 10). In stark contrast, Senge (1990) highlights the pivotal place that team learning has in a learning organization. His position is emphatic since he maintains that "unless teams can learn, the organization cannot learn" (p. 10).

Schmoker (1999) also refers to Lortie's notion of presentism: the "myriad of daily events and duties" (p. 10) that keeps teachers from reflecting collaboratively. However, as advocated by Schmoker and other writers cited by him, teamwork can counter this condition. This is supported by evidence he describes concerning the benefits of collaboration for students and teachers.

Individualism, isolationism, and presentism—exacerbated by the compartmentalized feature of schools—tend to inhibit the communication process in collaborative improvement efforts. Moreover, by its very nature, teaching is not a "team sport." Yet a common theme in school improvement literature regards collaboration as an essential factor in raising student achievement.

An implication of this theme for leadership is to provide a means to overcome obstacles to collaboration that would facilitate realizing the benefits of adopting a systems mentality. The provision for an evaluation team helps ensure that this outlook occurs. Thus in carrying out a program assessment, problems related to a lack of coordination regarding curricular processes among teachers can be identified. Information to remediate this deficiency can be obtained through a needs assessment. An instrument for this purpose is found in Chapter 7.

By conducting program assessments, holistic thinking should become more pervasive if teachers experience the satisfaction of seeing higher student achievement as a consequence of linking instructional efforts across grade levels and/or disciplines. Furthermore, this experience is heightened when the staff believes that they are a part of a school that is special— one that is continually improving—and that all have a role to play in this endeavor.[4] To this end, the attitude and actions of the principal and evaluation team are indispensable for creating an environment in which the potential of a learning organization can become realized. Carrying out their respective roles serves as a driving force that propels and sustains the work of school improvement.

APPLYING A SYSTEMS APPROACH TO INCREASE STUDENT ACHIEVEMENT

Actions that reflect systems thinking can be taken to raise student performance in that such actions have schoolwide implications. With this orientation, attempts should be made to minimize the risks associated with high-stakes testing for students and school personnel. What is needed here is to change the mentality of such testing so that the stakes, while regarded as important, are not perceived to be so high that students' anxiety levels detract from their performance. In short, mandated standardized testing should not take on a "do well or suffer the consequences" aura.[5] To prevent this counterproductive outlook, students need to be well prepared, beginning in the early grades, to perform competently on any exam. Underlying this goal is the belief on the part of students, teachers, and administrators that satisfactory (or even excellent) test scores are likely rather than doubtful. The following recommendations should help develop this conviction:

- Teachers across grade levels should hold continuous dialogues on ways to improve student achievement.

- Teachers in the higher grades should communicate to those teaching lower grades the knowledge and skills they have found to be most needed for students to meet higher grade requirements successfully.
- Teachers from the same grade level (or subject area) can exchange instructional techniques that they have found to be effective.
- Teachers can engage in collective problem solving, not only to enhance achievement, but also to remedy other areas that can affect academic performance such as behavior in and outside of the classroom. In this regard, McColskey and McMunn (2000) underscore the importance of collaboration for improving learning. They maintain that "in schools working toward instructional reform, administrators view teachers as professionals who need opportunities to work together to develop or fine-tune lessons, units, instructional materials, and assessment methods" (p. 119).
- Students should begin to develop test-taking skills early.
- These need to be taught throughout the grade levels.
- Practice standardized tests should be routinely administered.

Regarding the last point, this should help students get used to the experience of performing under the pressure of time and also gain familiarity with what is expected of them. Thus they would need to feel comfortable and confident[6] in a testing situation. When they are in this state, it would serve to lower unproductive anxiety and consequently free students to think more clearly. Furthermore, higher levels of confidence are likely to lead to greater perseverance and resiliency when more difficult material is presented.

Practice test taking provides for simulation, whereby students are able to rehearse their responses to the kinds of tasks they encounter in real situations. After these exams are scored, teachers will be in a position to know both the *type* and *extent* of deficiencies. Having this information is consistent with a performance mentality that coaches and performers themselves rely on. The benefit of such awareness finds expression in greater teaching effectiveness and efficiency in that remedial strategies can then be more focused using diagnostic data. With this orientation, the likelihood of overall improvement in student achievement is increased because instruction is not diluted by a more general approach.

Lending support to this point is Goldberg's (2005) citing of Popham's reference to "instructionally insensitive tests that most states use." Goldberg maintains that these tests do not help "figure out how to bring about improvement" (p. 390) because data are not broken down according to "the particular skill areas in which an individual student had weaknesses" (p. 390).[7] In the context of program evaluation, how such data can be analyzed is covered in Chapter 8.

As a further note, even if your state does report results by skill areas for certain subjects, it would be worthwhile to include in the evaluation those outcomes along with overall performance. This information would reveal the extent to which a program was *particularly* effective.

While the thrust of McColskey and McMunn's (2000) work argues for a long-term perspective of instructional reform, they also indicate what a school would "look like if educators focused exclusively on short-term fixes designed to boost test scores" (p. 116). Two of the short-term strategies they indicate are to administer practice tests and use computer programs "to enhance testing skills for students" (p. 117).[8]

The long-term strategy recommended by McColskey and McMunn (2000) of "providing students with meaningful and challenging work (not busy work)" (p. 118) is essential to developing individuals who are creative as well as effective problem solvers. However, the criterion for successful schools is still that which is most tangible to stakeholders—standardized test results. Thus educators need to survive the barrage of criticism leveled against lower performance in order to move in the direction advocated by McColskey and McMunn. In support of this point, McColskey, McCary, and Peel (as cited in McColskey & McMunn, 2000) maintain that

> while focusing on improving practice and quality will result in long-term improvement, short-term survival requires some attention be given to preparing students to perform on the type of state accountability test administered. However, addressing such a concern need not result in an exclusive preoccupation with raising test scores at any cost. Our approach has been to include not only test scores but also research-based instructional practices as the focus of dialogue with teachers and administrators to build a culture of inquiry. (p. 116)

Given this position, carrying out a program evaluation is congruous with the "culture of inquiry" inherent in a learning organization.

Connecting Program Evaluation, the Learning Organization, and High-Stakes Test Preparation

Inherent in a learning organization is the disposition on the part of its members to learn from the work they do and correspondingly improve their competencies. Thus in this type of setting, people "are continually learning how to learn together" (Senge, 1990, p. 3). In this environment, when program evaluation is carried out so that different grade levels or departments participate in assessment projects over time, these endeavors can contribute to a school's development as a better performing entity. Therefore an evaluation of a curriculum will determine if it is functioning effectively or if not, what changes are called for to make it so. Moreover, if these changes are found to work well, the basic structure of the curriculum itself may not have to be modified that much, if at all. With a well-designed program in place, this situation can contribute to teacher productivity since its instructional activities enhance the explanation of concepts and principles and its follow-up assignments reinforce what students need to master.

High-stakes test preparation enters into the relationship of a learning organization and program evaluation. In this regard, when a needs assessment is incorporated into an evaluation scheme (as discussed in Chapter 7), this can elicit suggestions regarding actions that should be taken to prepare students for high-stakes tests or to raise their performance on any other indicator. When such actions are taken, aligned with the mentality of a learning organization, teachers and administrators gain knowledge they would consider practical. Thus they can see directly what helps them do their jobs better, as evidenced by the payoff of increased student achievement.

A CONCLUDING NOTE

Integrating formative and summative methods is consistent with reflective practice engaged in by members of a learning organization.[9] School personnel who function in this environment recognize that both types of assessment enhance their thinking about how student achievement can be raised. Thus formative and summative information stimulate dialogues concerning (a) the reasons why certain instructional activities are more effective than others and (b) ways in which future efforts of program delivery can be refined. These discussions bring an overriding sense of fulfillment when the learning organization moves inexorably forward, driven by the momentum of success that a systems approach to school improvement can engender.[10]

CHAPTER 2 HIGHLIGHTS

1. Program evaluation regularly carried out is a natural feature of a school as a learning organization because it provides a mechanism whereby its members can gain insights about which aspects of the curriculum produced the best learning conditions and which aspects need to be strengthened.

2. The various phases of an evaluation project—from planning its design, to collecting and analyzing data, drawing conclusions, and offering recommendations for improvement—requires systematic thought.

3. Searching for a solution to a problem is facilitated through a program evaluation project. Its activities are oriented systematically and comprehensively toward addressing a problem.

4. Problems are indispensable for personal and professional growth because their solutions often require creative approaches, and these can constitute curriculum modifications that increase student motivation and learning.

5.   A structure for taking appropriate actions by the school as a learning organization is the evaluation team. The work of the team is greatly enhanced when the members of the organization at all levels adopt a systems mentality. This perspective is an overriding aspect of the learning organization as conceptualized by Senge (1990).

6.   Systems thinking (Senge, 1990) is sound since individuals can better understand the interconnectiveness of their work in the school organization. This insight facilitates higher organizational performance by bringing collective wisdom, produced through reflective practice, to bear on problems that prevent curricular processes from functioning optimally, thereby restricting student outcomes.

7.   In carrying out program assessment, problems related to a lack of coordination regarding curricular processes among teachers can be identified and remediated.

8.   Students need to be well prepared, beginning in the early grades, to perform competently on any exam. Underlying this goal is the belief on the part of students, teachers, and administrators that satisfactory (or even excellent) test scores are likely rather than doubtful.

9.   High-stakes test preparation enters into the relationship of a learning organization and program evaluation.

10. In an environment of a learning organization, school personnel recognize that, consistent with reflective practice, both formative and summative evaluation methods enhance their thinking about how student achievement can be raised.

NOTES

1. Although Burns (1978) used the term *transforming leadership*, it is more commonly referred to as *transformational leadership*.

2. Fitzpatrick et al. (2004) cite the work of Preskill and Torres in pointing out that evaluation conducted in a learning organization "can be used to educate and change the views and skills of various groups" (p. 177).

3. Based on Kanter's (1983) conception of companies that have segmentalist cultures, i.e., that is characterized by compartmentalized structures, DuFour and Eaker (1992) indicate that this type of culture describes many school districts.

4. Sergiovanni (1999) points out the motivating effect that occurs when members of the school organization (including students) feel that they belong to something special.

5. Calling attention to the negative consequences of high-stakes testing is a common theme of the literature on this topic.

6. Stiggins (2002) makes the point that classroom assessments can be used "to *build students' confidence* in themselves as learners" (p. 761).

7. Citing Goldberg's position should not be construed as criticism of these tests because in fairness they are designed for summative, not formative purposes.

8. These authors also raise questions about having every teacher overdo instruction of test-taking skills.

9. With respect to organizational learning, Weiss (1998) discusses one of the purposes of evaluation—that of providing feedback to enable the staff to reflect upon improving practice. From the work of Schön, she indicates that a canny administrator may find that encouraging reflective practice is desirable.

10. Although not in the context of discussing school improvement, Csikszentmihalyi (as cited in Schmoker, 1999), maintains that the sense of moving forward as well as psychic satisfaction are provided by steady growth.

Using Program Evaluation to Improve the Curriculum— A Developmental Approach

This chapter discusses how nonexperimental and experimental program evaluation[1] provide a developmental and complementary approach to improve a curriculum. Based on the results obtained from nonexperimental research, a faculty can modify an existing program and assess changes. This calls for conducting program evaluation through experimentation. Accordingly, concepts and factors to consider in carrying out this type of investigation are covered. This information serves as background material for Chapter 4 in which experimental methodology is treated in greater depth.

COMPATIBLE EVALUATION METHODS

Consistent with the growth concept of kaizen, evaluation carried out for the purpose of improving school achievement strengthens the link that connects the assessment results, the curriculum's ongoing development, and progressively higher student performance. In this vein, an ongoing program should be a dynamic entity, constantly evolving. Apropos to this notion is DuFour and Eaker's (1992) point that school improvement efforts are endless. They would be, since achieving excellence in program outcomes involves a building process that, with each improvement, reveals discoveries of what students and teachers can accomplish.

Given this assumption, the quality of a program and its impact is enhanced when direction for its improvement is rooted in the best thinking of practitioners who systematically and comprehensively have tested their prescription for a more promising way to deliver instruction. To this end, program evaluation can be considered from two time perspectives—past and future. Each involves a different methodology that can be classified as either nonexperimental or experimental research.

Nonexperimental Program Evaluation

When assessing a program that is currently in operation (e.g., a regular curriculum), the time orientation is "past" or looking back. That is, the program has been operating for some time, and the investigators now want to gather evidence regarding various dimensions of its effectiveness and related instructional processes.

This type of evaluation analyzes data with respect to judging the program as it now stands—prior to making any changes and can thereby be classified under the umbrella of nonexperimental research. Such inquiry is important because it provides a rationale for introducing changes in the curriculum, which are later tested experimentally. Thus both nonexperimental and experimental research are complementary from a curriculum development point of view.

Experimental Program Evaluation

In contrast to the nonexperimental method, a future time perspective is taken by conducting an experiment in which a modified or an innovative program[2] is evaluated to determine its impact. For this endeavor, a change based on consensus is introduced and, after waiting for a period of time (e.g., one year), the extent of progress to date can be evaluated.[3]

Terms and Principles Associated with the Experimental Method

In carrying out this type of study, researchers *manipulate the independent variable*. This means that groups are treated differently; that is, each is provided with distinct learning activities. An independent variable consists of two or more treatments (or methods),[4] for example, different instructional programs, one of which could have a greater influence on the outcome than the other. Thus it is useful to make the connection between the INdependent variable and INfluence.

Students who receive the modified or innovative program comprise the experimental group, while those who are exposed to the regular program form the control group. The latter serves as the frame of reference for comparing the effectiveness of the experimental treatment or condition.

The *dependent variable* is also known as the outcome variable (or just outcome). This variable reflects differences in scores or other measures obtained from both groups. Thus the extent of these differences between the groups depends on the impact of a part of the independent variable, that is, a particular method or program. Put another way, the dependent variable also reveals the results of the treatments.

Note that there can be an independent and dependent variable in nonexperimental as well as experimental research. However, the major characteristic that differentiates the two methods is the manipulation feature of the experimental approach. (Features of both types of research as applied to program evaluation are shown in Figure 3.1.)

The main advantage of experimental over nonexperimental research is that more control can be exercised over outside factors that can affect the outcome in addition to (or besides) the experimental treatment. The reason for this is that when a program that has been in operation for a period of time is being evaluated, factors that could have enhanced its results in addition to the impact of the curriculum itself may have already occurred. In this sense, these factors cannot be "undone." Consider two examples: (a) during the past year, an outstanding teacher has implemented the program, or (b) the class participating in the program being assessed contained a larger than usual number of above average students. Would this program have been as effective without these advantages? This question would be better answered by an experiment because these types of advantages could be controlled for when *planning* the research. In this regard, both experimental and control groups would be balanced by influencing factors that were not part of each program. How this can be done is covered in Chapter 4.

Figure 3.1 Comparing Experimental and Nonexperimental Methods as Applied to Program Evaluation

Feature	Experimental	Nonexperimental
Time orientation—Past		•
Time orientation—Future		•
Manipulate the independent variable	•	
More control of extraneous variables	•	
Conduct formative and summative evaluation	•	•
Use of dependent (outcome) variables to measure results	•	•
Improve program based on results	•	•

THE PROBLEM OF CONFOUNDING

When one or more outside factors have exerted influence, this undesirable occurrence is termed *confounding*. This situation is present when the combined influence of a treatment with one or more *extraneous* variables causes a noticeable difference in favor of the experimental group. These variables are considered extraneous because they are not part of the experiment. The problem here is that they could also affect the outcome. In fact, they can exert an even greater influence than a particular treatment. For example, students in the experimental group may have received more tutoring, or that group's teacher could have obtained additional professional knowledge during the course of the experiment. Such advantages could have boosted the achievement of students in the experimental group in addition to the treatment they received.

Under such circumstances, it would not be possible to determine how much of the differences (technically known as *variance*) in achievement could be attributed to the experimental treatment and how much could be accounted for by extraneous factors. Thus confounding is present because there would be confusion when interpreting the results.[5]

Unplanned events such as those indicated may not be the only factors that could produce confounding. Other factors can also threaten the *internal validity* of experimental findings, as discussed next.

INTERNAL VALIDITY

This type of validity refers to a situation where it can be reasonably concluded that the experimental treatment was solely responsible for any differences and did not act in combination with a factor extraneous to the planned intervention, that is, the innovative program.[6] Unplanned, outside events (those not part of the experimental treatment) constitute unwanted influence and are labeled "history." It is one of a number of threats that lessen internal validity. More are examined later in this chapter.

History

This threat is so named because, during the course or history of the experiment, an event occurred that, together with a particular treatment, could have produced the outcome. For example, students in the experimental group may have gone on more field trips, heard invited speakers, or read additional interesting books recommended by their teacher. These activities could have increased student motivation.

At the time summative evidence is collected, it is not possible to eliminate the effect of history since the event has already taken place. In an attempt to prevent this situation, the evaluation team should explain to those delivering the innovative program the problem of including learning activities that were not part of the modifications being tested. This should be done during the planning stage of the experiment. However, if, for any reason, the teachers of the experimental group would want to incorporate the ancillary approach as part of the program, then this change should be noted in the evaluation report when results of the experiment are discussed. The reason for this is that if the experimental group is higher on all indicators, as compared to the control group, the difference between them may not be accounted for solely by the teaching/learning activities of the intervention that were originally planned.

Given the potential confounding effect of additional factors, teachers should agree to implement the program as newly designed.[7] On the other hand, during the course of the experiment, teachers in the experimental group may want to include other learning activities and materials that they feel can improve student achievement. If, in their professional judgment, these should be used in the future when the program is presented again, then this change should be encouraged.

When alterations are made, the faculty of the innovative program should provide the team with a written description of these. Modifications consistent with the goals of a program are in keeping with collecting formative data since the purpose of such data is to improve the operation of the program.

Not all unplanned events could motivate the program's faculty to make changes based on them. An extraneous factor over which the evaluators have no control could occur. For example, during the experimental period, a new department head may be appointed and bring to this role a vision of the program's potential, as well as providing enthusiastic support for it. This could have an energizing effect on those teaching in the program that may result in higher student outcomes.

There could be a situation in which an outside event could disadvantage the control group, thereby giving the experimental group an edge. For example, assume that there are two faculty members involved in an experiment. One teaches in the innovative program, the other in the regular curriculum; both have teacher aides. During the course of the experiment, a principal reassigns the aide from the regular curriculum—who happens to be experienced—to a new teacher who is not part of the experiment.

The replacement aide, though well intentioned, has not taken the initiative as did her predecessor, nor was she as skilled. As a result, the teacher has not been able to individualize instruction to the extent that she did before because she has to do more follow-up of learning activities on her own. Thus the students have not received as much attention according to their deficiencies. In this situation, if the students in the experimental group out perform those in the regular program, the difference may not be a function of the intervention, but may be due to the control group being handicapped by not receiving as much individualized attention. Without this unexpected event of the change of aides, the achievement of the regular students may have been comparable to, or perhaps even surpassed, that of those in the innovative program.

Selection

Another threat to internal validity is referred to as selection. This describes the case where the innovative program has, for example, a noticeably larger percentage of higher achieving and/or fewer problem behavior students at the beginning of the experiment. This imbalance gives a decided advantage to the innovative group if the outcomes are in its favor.

Attrition

The loss of participants in an experiment, known as attrition, threatens internal validity because these students are not available to provide summative assessment data. One of the reasons for attrition is that participants could have moved from the school. If both experimental and control groups are relatively small (e.g., an experiment involving only two classes), this threat could be a factor in accounting for any difference in, for example, test performance. Thus attrition could favor the experimental group if input cannot be included from lower achieving students in this group and/or if better achievers in the control group were not present to contribute summative information.

Demoralization

Another situation that could be advantageous to students participating in the innovative program would be the demoralization of students in the regular program. It refers to a lower level of esprit for this group, thereby affecting the motivation of its members because they feel that they have not been selected to participate in the innovative program. The problem could be exacerbated if students in the control group were also in the same school as those in the experimental group.

Preventing or minimizing the potential for demoralization falls within the scope of the leadership role in program development. Thus the principal should be cautious about elevating the status and prestige of faculty members and students in the innovative program. Being overly laudatory about their activities could send an unintentional message to the control group that somehow its efforts are just ordinary—not exciting, state of the art, or special. Making a group feel special in some way could also pose an internal validity threat since one would not be able to disentangle positive outcomes from the effects of boosts to the collective ego of the experimental group.

John Henry Effect

Instead of the control group being demoralized because it was not selected to receive the innovative program, its teacher may regard the experimental class as rivals. Consequently, the control group teacher, in a competitive spirit, could strive harder to make his or her students perform even better than those receiving the intervention.[8] This feeling of rivalry and related behavior is known as the John Henry effect after the legendary railroad worker who competed against a machine. In this regard, if the compensatory efforts of the regular teacher are successful, they may mask the effectiveness of the innovative program.

Experimenter Effect

This effect can present another handicap for the intervention if those implementing the program do not carry it out as planned. An example would be modifying the time allowed for certain learning activities. In contrast to the John Henry effect, the experimenter effect can work in *favor* of the intervention. In this situation, those implementing the innovation may exert extra effort in an attempt to have the program succeed. Another manifestation of a positive experimenter effect would be teacher enthusiasm—a potent and contagious factor in any learning situation. Its influence may be revealed in greater student motivation and subsequent higher achievement. Since the experimenter effect could combine with the activities of the program, it poses another threat to internal validity.

SOME FURTHER THREATS TO INTERNAL VALIDITY

An experiment can still be conducted even if it is not possible or practical to obtain a control group. This situation highlights the need for investigators to be particularly mindful of factors that could combine with the treatment if the experimental group shows noticeable improvement. Thus in addition to threats already discussed, the presence of others can raise the issue of whether findings are valid. However, a control group provides the same opportunity for extraneous variables to affect student outcomes in both the intervention and regular programs. Put another way, factors not part of the experimental treatment are assumed to be reasonably balanced across both groups. This enables the intervention to be judged on its own merits. The following are additional threats to internal validity that should be considered, especially when using a one-group design.

Maturation

This refers to the normal growth of students over time as a factor contributing to the outcome in addition to that produced by the intervention. Such growth encompasses cognitive, social, and emotional development.

Instrumentation

A change in the way students are measured on a posttest could facilitate their performance. For example, when compared to a pretest, if the directions on a posttest are made clearer or some of its items revised, it may make it easier for students to demonstrate their knowledge and/or ability. This would then be reflected by higher test performance of the group.

Pretesting

Taking a test at the beginning of an experiment could alert students to the major topics that will be covered in the future. Believing that they will be tested again at a later date, the students may focus their studying on the various topics they have remembered from the pretest. This could boost performance on the posttest in addition to the learning activities of the innovative program. The threat of pretesting could therefore sensitize students to what is important to master. Pretesting could be a factor, especially for the more motivated students who could internalize the cues provided by the pretest. On the other hand, since students are routinely tested, pretesting may not be a concern. However, if the extent of improvement is being measured as an indicator of program effectiveness, then the evaluators have no choice but to include data from the pretest, whether or not one or two groups are involved in the experiment.

Figure 3.2   Various Threats to Internal Validity That Can Artificially Boost an Innovative Program's Effectiveness

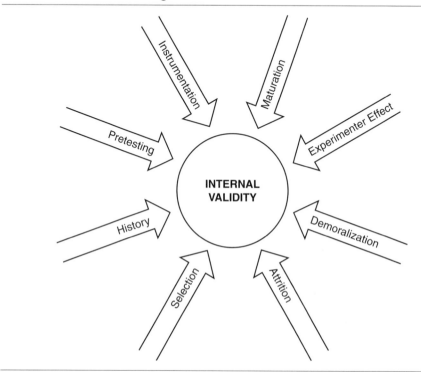

A Further Perspective on Experimental Methodology

As is apparent from reading this chapter, there is a fair amount of technical information involved in conducting an experiment. This will also be evident in Chapter 4. Why then is learning this material relevant given the fact that teachers are not professional researchers? Because as reiterated in some form or another in this book, the guidelines are designed to help practitioners assess programs to determine the extent to which they are functional. Such research needs to be carried out in a sound way in order to give the modified or pilot program a fair chance to demonstrate its potential. If the results reveal that students in the experimental program achieved noticeably higher than those in the control group, and the study has been conducted systematically, this supports the case for adopting the curriculum being tested.

A CONCLUDING NOTE

As stated earlier, confounding is present when the results of an intervention appear to be effective, but it cannot be stated with sufficient confidence that the success was due solely to the experimental program (see Figure 3.2). Thus threats to internal validity prevent a more definite judgment about the effectiveness of a program. If, however, these threats could be controlled, conclusions can then be drawn with greater assurance. Methods for achieving control in an experimental study are discussed in Chapter 4.

CHAPTER 3 HIGHLIGHTS

1.   Evaluation carried out for the purpose of improving school achievement strengthens the link that connects assessment results, the curriculum's ongoing development, and progressively higher student performance.

2.   When the decision is made to assess a program that has been in operation (e.g., a regular curriculum), then the time orientation is "past." This approach involves a nonexperimental method of research.

3.   With an experimental program evaluation, research is conducted to determine the impact of a modified or an innovative program that is assessed at a future date.

4.   In carrying out an experiment, researchers manipulate the independent variable. This means that groups are treated differently; that is, each is provided with distinct learning activities.

5.   The innovative program is given to the students in the experimental group; those in the regular program constitute the control group.

6. The **dependent variable** is also known as the outcome variable. This variable reflects differences in scores or other measures obtained from the groups.

7. The main advantage of experimental over nonexperimental research is that more control can be exercised over outside factors (**extraneous variables**) that can affect the outcome besides (or in addition to) the experimental treatment.

8. If it is not possible to determine how much of the differences in an outcome variable could be attributed to the experimental treatment and how much could be accounted for by extraneous factors, **confounding** is present. This would lead to confusion when interpreting results.

9. **Internal validity** refers to a situation where it can be reasonably concluded that the experimental treatment was solely responsible for any differences in the outcome and did not act in combination with any extraneous variables.

10. The following extraneous variables can artificially boost an innovative program's effectiveness: history, selection, attrition, demoralization of students in the control group, experimenter effect, maturation, instrumentation, and pretesting.

11. Controlling threats to internal validity enables conclusions to be drawn about the effectiveness of the intervention with greater confidence.

12. If results reveal that students in an experimental program achieved noticeably higher than those in the control group, and the study has been conducted systematically, this strengthens the case for adopting the curriculum being tested.

NOTES

1. The term experimental evaluation is used by Fink (1995) and is used in the same way in this chapter. In contrast to this method, her discussion of program evaluation designs points out the well-established principle that when a method has been implemented for some time, there is less control over factors that could also influence its results. The example Fink uses, similar to the one in this chapter, refers to the issue of whether a program was effective given the possibility that all "high scorers were more knowledgeable to begin with" (p. 70). Her descriptions of retrospective and prospective approaches to program evaluation are consistent with the nonexperimental and experimental assessment methods described in this chapter. Regarding the former method, Posavac and Carey (2007) refer to single-group program evaluations as nonexperimental. These authors illustrate different approaches to this type of assessment. In terms of time, one involves a past orientation that is congruent with the nonexperimental method discussed in this chapter. However, this method, as covered later in the book, can involve comparisons between two groups.

2. The terms *modified and innovative program* as well as *intervention* are used synonymously in this book.

3. After the present program has been assessed, a decision may be made to experiment with an entirely new program, rather than modify the current offering. This action would still be consistent with taking a developmental perspective in seeking a potentially more effective curriculum.

4. While an independent variable can involve more than two treatments, in this book references are made to either a one- or two-group situation.

5. Suter (1998) also describes confounding as results that are confusing to interpret.

6. The notion of internal validity and how certain factors can threaten it was developed by Campbell and Stanley (1963). The material in this section discussing such factors is based largely on their classic work.

7. The control group teacher(s) should also agree not to modify instruction. The reason for this is that altering usual learning activities for students in the control group changes the original comparison. In this regard, if the achievement of these students is higher as a result, the modifications could make the innovative program appear less effective.

8. If there is more than one teacher in the regular program, the other instructor(s) could also contribute to the John Henry effect.

4

An Experimental Approach for Evaluating Programs

This chapter extends the discussion of describing the methodology for conducting an experiment. First, the technical aspects of controlling extraneous variables are covered, followed by the use of different experimental designs. Issues in using a control group are also discussed. The chapter further points out the importance of being able to generalize the results of a program evaluation to apply to future students who would participate in the program.

INTERNAL VALIDITY—A REVIEW

Recall that when an experiment has internal validity this means that the experimental treatment itself (the innovative program) has produced a successful outcome unaided by one or more extraneous variables. Such variables involve factors that should not be part of any treatment given to the experimental and control groups and, therefore, must be controlled. If these factors are not controlled, this situation leads to confusion when interpreting results. Technically, confounding is present since one would not know if an outcome in favor of the innovative program (e.g., higher test scores) could be attributed to the treatment it received, the extraneous variable(s), or a combination of both influences.

BUILDING CONTROL INTO AN EXPERIMENT

In order to control extraneous variables, nontreatment conditions (e.g., years of teaching experience) that can also have an effect on the outcomes are held constant. To achieve this, a control group is used. As previously indicated, this provision enables the impact of nontreatment factors to be reasonably balanced across the innovative and regular programs. Therefore, both groups have the same opportunity to be similarly affected by extraneous variables. The only variable that should not be held constant is, of course, the independent variable, that is the different programs being compared.

It should be pointed out that even with a control group, it is still possible for an unplanned event to take place that could benefit the experimental treatment. For example, as noted earlier, more students in the innovative program may have received tutoring than did those in the regular program. Except for this type of situation, having conditions that can affect both experimental and control groups in similar ways puts evaluators in a position to conclude more definitely that an innovative program was responsible for better results (if these in fact occurred) since nontreatment influences were controlled. Stated another way, this conclusion can be drawn since factors that could affect outcomes besides the treatments were held constant for the experimental and control groups.

When it can be reasonably concluded that better student outcomes can be linked to the innovative rather than the regular program, then the experiment can be considered as having internal validity. Thus the control group has served a valuable function by providing data as a frame of reference against which outcomes from the innovative program can be compared.

Planning an Experiment

To control for extraneous variables, think of the "level playing field" metaphor: Set up conditions so that the "game" can be played fairly. This cannot be done if the intervention has situational advantages over the regular program. To prevent this, the following factors should be as similar as possible for both the experimental and control groups at the beginning of the experiment:

- Composition of the groups with respect to such factors as achievement level, behavioral problem students, socioeconomic level, and gender
- Experience and qualifications of teachers
- Time of day programs are offered
- Physical environment of the classrooms
- Material to be covered
- Tests and other outcome measures to be used

Figure 4.1 synthesizes major points concerning the concept of internal validity. It is interesting to note how the prefix **CON-** links these concepts.

Figure 4.1   Achieving Internal Validity in an Experiment: Confirming if the Experimental Treatment Itself Was Effective

---

Results that cannot be disentangled from the influence of extraneous variables on an experimental treatment are confusing.

- **CON**fusing results are termed **CON**founding.

- Prevent **CON**founding by keeping nontreatment **CON**ditions **CON**stant for the experimental and control groups.

- When **CON**founding is not present, **CON**clusions about the effectiveness of the experimental treatment can be drawn more **CON**vincingly.

Issues to consider when using a control group in an evaluation study are examined later. At this point, it would be useful to discuss random assignment—a control mechanism that can be applied to make the groups comparable.

RANDOM ASSIGNMENT

When random assignment is used, the total number of subjects (students) that will participate in the experiment are divided to form the experimental and control groups. This process is based on chance (e.g., the flip of a coin) not on the judgment of the person(s) responsible for planning the evaluation. The rationale for this is that an objective means is used to form the groups rather than a subjective opinion about who should be assigned to each program. The problem with relying on personal judgment is that, although not intentional, it may favor the experimental group.

Random assignment allows one to assume that both groups are equal (or nearly so) at the start of the experiment. This applies to any student variable that can affect the outcome besides the treatments, for example, prior achievement and/or motivational level. The basis for this assumption is that students who are high and low on certain characteristics will be balanced evenly between the groups. However, randomization does *not guarantee* that the students in both programs are comparable at the beginning. Even after the groups have been formed by this process, the regular program may still be disadvantaged because it has, for example, more students with a history of poor classroom behavior. Conversely, the experimental group may hold the advantage if it contains a larger percentage of better students. Therefore, when more students with a certain characteristic are found in one of the groups, these particular students should be reassigned randomly so that the composition of the programs is comparable. Figure 4.2 summarizes what can and cannot be achieved by using random assignment.

Figure 4.2 Random Assignment: A Method of Experimental Control

It does	**It does not**
form experimental and control groups objectively, by chance.	rely on subjective judgment to form groups.
assume that at the beginning of the experiment both groups are equal—or nearly so—on any student variable that can affect an outcome.	guarantee that the experimental and control groups will be comparable at the beginning of the experiment.

The Use of Matching

Random assignment can be used in conjunction with matching to add further control since this provides greater assurance that students in both groups would be similar on a variable that could affect the outcome. Figure 4.3 lists the steps involved to integrate both processes.

Figure 4.3 Combining Random Assignment with Matching

1. Use a measure that currently indicates students' achievement levels prior to the beginning of the experiment (e.g., the results of a standardized test).

2. Form two subgroups based on gender, and rank students from high to low in each one.

3. Taking one subgroup, pair the top two students, then the next two, and so on. Flip a coin; let heads and tails represent the experimental and control groups respectively. If heads appears, the first student in the pair is assigned to the experimental group; the other automatically goes to the control group. If tails, the first student goes to the control group and the other to the experimental group.

4. Repeat the process for each succeeding pair until there are no more left for that subgroup. Use the same method for the second subgroup.

5. If one student is left over from each subgroup, flip a coin to determine group assignment; do the same if there is only one student and no match.

A Note on Random Assignment

While this process is designed to equalize the groups, its use may not be feasible. Obviously, if the school year is in progress, classes cannot be re-formed for the sake of testing a program. The potential for negative reactions from parents, teachers, and students would not be worth it even if an innovative program appears promising. Thus random assignment is more practical when fall classes are being scheduled in the summer.

There are other limitations to randomization:

- In smaller schools there may be only one class at a particular grade level.
- The process cannot work if two schools are to separately represent the experimental and control groups.

Despite these limitations, random assignment can help control the possible influence of extraneous variables. However, its use raises an ethical issue since students in the control group would not be the beneficiaries of a potentially more effective program. From another perspective, with reference to random assignment, Fitzpatrick et al. (2004) pose the question of whether it is ethical to expose people to a program that may be less successful than the current one.[1]

To lessen the probability of this situation occurring calls upon the disposition of administrators and faculty to continually seek better ways to deliver instruction. This quest enhances professional development as personnel learn from their efforts. In turn, such knowledge can help raise student achievement.[2]

It really does not matter by which means (random assignment or consensus) it is decided who will receive the intervention; the potential inequity of this determination is still a consideration. This problem is always present when a pilot program involves only certain students. Yet, unless a school experiments with potentially promising programs, students overall will not benefit as much. Another way to look at this is that if the modified program is successful, then former students in the control group could benefit if changes reflecting improvement in delivery of course content in the same subject were incorporated into a program they would subsequently take.

EXPERIMENTAL DESIGNS

These designs[3] can be thought of as a scheme for planning a study in which two groups or a single group will participate. The first design, shown in Figure 4.4, incorporates the use of random assignment, symbolized by RA.

Figure 4.4 Randomized Pretest-Posttest Control Group

	Group	Measurement I	Treatment	Measurement 2
RA	Experimental	Pretest	Innovative program	Posttest
	Control	Pretest	Regular program	Posttest

This design has three functions:

- It measures the extent of improvement of each group over time. (Typically, the mean difference is used to determine change.)
- The use of random assignment controls the threats of selection, maturation, pretesting, and instrumentation because each group has the same opportunity to be affected by these extraneous variables.
- The pretest provides a check on whether groups are initially equivalent (or nearly so) on a variable that could affect the outcome in addition to the experimental treatment.

Recall that with random assignment one could assume that the groups were equal to begin with on any student factor, such as ability and attitudes that could influence the results. However, if it is not feasible to randomize participants since classes are already formed and if a control group is still to be used, then the design in Figure 4.5 would be appropriate.

Figure 4.5   Nonrandomized Pretest-Posttest Control Group

Group	Measurement I	Treatment	Measurement 2
Experimental	Pretest	Innovative program	Posttest
Control	Pretest	Regular program	Posttest

With this design, one can only determine if groups are equal on the pretest and not assume that they are equal on other variables, as is the case when random assignment is used. Notwithstanding this caveat, assuming that conditions under which the experiment is conducted are comparable, the nonrandomized design still provides a practical way of comparing the relative effectiveness of both treatments. The reason for this is that, as discussed earlier in this chapter, extraneous variables can be controlled in planning the experiment.

If only one group will participate in the experiment, due, for example, to ethical or practical reasons (Suter, 1998), or if only one group is available, then the design shown in Figure 4.6 can be used.

Figure 4.6   One-Group Time Series

Pretest I	Pretest 2	/ Intervention /	Posttest I	Posttest 2

The one-group time series design provides a way to determine the *consistency* of measures obtained before and after the intervention has taken place.[4] If, however, only one measure had been taken prior to introducing the intervention, student test performance may be lower than usual. This could be due to a number of reasons such as interruptions during the day, illness, or the test being administered by a substitute teacher. Lower achievement on a pretest can make the effect of an intervention appear more dramatic and thereby give a false impression of its impact. Thus having at least two measures can alert the evaluators to a marked discrepancy between them. If this occurs, the higher mean should be used. When the measures are close in value, the one nearest in time to the intervention provides the baseline data.

The advantage of a second posttest is that it measures the *stability* of the effects of the intervention. However, if only one posttest were given and scores declined for reasons such as those mentioned previously, this would mask the influence of the experimental treatment and lead to a conclusion biased against it.

As indicated in Figure 4.7, scheduling each pair of tests within a month seems reasonable. However, the decision regarding the time frame for testing should be made by the evaluation team and the program faculty. Moreover, alternative forms of the tests should be used, if possible, to minimize the opportunity for students to answer an item simply because they remembered it from the previous test.

Figure 4.7   Sample Schedule for a One-Group Time Series Design

Pretest 1	Pretest 2	/ Intervention /	Posttest 1	Posttest 2
Early September	Late September		Early May	Late May

To check on the durability of the treatment, follow-up testing could also be done in the fall, after the students have moved on to the next grade, since the program would not have been operating during the summer.

A Note on Using a One-Group Design

Since this design does not provide for including a comparison group, the only basis for judgment is the extent of growth from pre- to posttest. However, the change may also be due to the influence of one or more extraneous variables. It is, therefore, important to substantiate any evidence of noticeable improvement with the judgment of those who have implemented the innovative program. These faculty members, because of their everyday experiences with students, are in the best position to assess if marked progress has been made. They can express their opinions by answering open-ended questions that elicit more in-depth information from respondents concerning the program's impact. This is in contrast to using a format in which respondents are asked to indicate their opinions by checking a scale with several categories such as "very effective" through "not very effective." (How evaluation data can be collected by posing open-ended questions is discussed in Chapter 7.) The following are examples of the types of questions that should be used when a program involving only a single group is being assessed. (These are also appropriate for two-group designs.)

- How effective is the current program in raising reading achievement? Please explain.
- How would you compare the current program's effectiveness with the one previously used?

It may be the case that no students in the school are available to serve as a control group, or it may be decided that the program should be open to all those eligible because no one should be denied its potential benefits. Given these possibilities, a principal might be able to obtain the cooperation of another school similar in student population that would function as a control group. However, the use of a second school raises logistical issues with respect to such aspects as coordinating class content, tests, surveys with the staff, and scheduling experimental activities. Moreover, it may be difficult to find a school comparable on other factors besides student indicators (e.g., teachers with experience similar to those in the innovative program, principal's leadership style, and school climate). Such factors are realities to consider when asking another school to cooperate. In this regard, the more that experimental and control schools are dissimilar, the more tentative should be the conclusions drawn regarding the intervention's effectiveness. Thus while there is less control of extraneous variables in a one-group design, paradoxically, there is more control of the logistics of carrying out an evaluation when the assessment involves only one school.

DECIDING WHETHER TO USE ONE OR TWO GROUPS IN AN EVALUATION STUDY

While a two-group design controls conditions better and also provides a basis for a current comparison, this does not suggest that using only one group would result in an unsound assessment. Even if a single group design raises one or more of the issues discussed earlier, the program should still be evaluated. However, as indicated previously, with one group the need to obtain corroborative evidence to provide a basis of comparison is underscored. Thus if the students in the innovative program have characteristics similar to participants that experienced a different program the previous year, then their respective percentages of improvement can be compared.

It should also be mentioned that comparing a current group's performance with that of a previous one makes conclusions more tentative. The conditions under which the programs were operating could have been markedly dissimilar, such as differences between teachers in years' experience and instructional style and differences in parental support and cooperation. This situation highlights the importance of having a teacher in the innovative program judge it relative to the one that he or she taught in the past.

As an aid to deciding whether to use one or two groups, features of the designs discussed are synthesized in Figure 4.8.

Figure 4.8 Features of Experimental Designs

Design	Used When	What It Does
Randomized Pretest–Posttest Control Group	Students can be randomly assigned to experimental and control groups before school begins.	• Measures improvement • Random assignment controls for internal valididty threats of selection, maturation, pre-testing, and instrumentation • With random assignment it can be assumed that groups were equal on any student variable that can influence results • Pretest provides a check on wheter groups are iniitially equivalent on a variable that could affect the outcome • Controls by providing for comparable nontreatment conditions
Nonrandomized Pretest-Posttest Control Group	Intact classes representing the experimental and control groups are being compared	• Measures improvement • Determines if groups were equal on a pretest • Controls by providing for comparable nontreatment conditions
One-Group Time Series	A comparison is not being made with a control group	• Measures improvement • Additional pre- and post-tests determine if measures obtained before and after the intervention has taken place were consistent.

EXTERNAL VALIDITY

The extent to which a program has applicability for future students is an-other essential issue that needs to be taken into account in evaluating a program. This involves judging the extent to which other students similar to those participating in the intervention would benefit, provided, of course, that the treatment was found to be effective. Thus if teachers be-lieve that the students in the innovative program are typical of those who would participate in the future, then similar results can also be expected to occur for prospective students. Projecting the findings of the intervention to others refers to the experiment's *external validity* since conclusions can be extended, that is, generalized, beyond the current investigation (Campbell & Stanley, 1963).

If, however, any situational factors, for example, the threat of history, gave an advantage to the innovative program, external validity would be lessened. Such an occurrence would make the program less applicable for replication because the outside factor was not part of the program. A future frame of reference is congruent with the evolutionary aspect of program development. This lens conveys an optimistic perspective since it anticipates the promise that the program holds in terms of processes and outcomes for students as well as faculty.

Formative Evaluation Applied to Experimental Studies

Based on a summative evaluation, if changes are made to a program then a formative assessment should be carried out to monitor how well the modified version is being implemented. This determination can be conducted informally and collaboratively by the staff members delivering it.

The basic idea of formative evaluation is to obtain information to guide decisions about improving a program. With respect to the one that has been modified, it should be treated as a newly adopted program. Therefore, consistent with a formative focus, it would be examined in its "early" stages of operation to determine if and how changes should be made. The point here is not to wait too long before minor glitches or deficiencies handicap the delivery of the program. In this regard, with respect to formative evaluation, Fitzpatrick et al. (2004) raise the caveat that information received too late for use in improving a program is "patently useless."

In efforts to prevent this situation, consistent with the team learning feature of a learning organization, faculty members should engage in dialogues (Senge, 1990) concerning how the program is functioning. When to begin these discussions should be established by the program staff and held regularly until the experiment is well on its way.

In reflective practice fashion, formative assessment of the program by the staff members involves raising issues concerning conditions that affect their teaching. To elicit these perspectives, the following questions[5] can be used to provide a framework for discussion. The staff may also want to raise other issues.

- What is working well thus far? How do we know this? (For these questions, in addition to teachers' opinions, student performance on tests and other assignments should be considered.)
- Should any of the modifications be improved? If "yes," how?
- Should any other parts of the curriculum be improved besides the modifications? If "yes," how?

- Beyond the curriculum itself, what, if anything, do we need to help ensure that the program is operating effectively? (For this question, the staff would consider the need for more training [Fitzpatrick et al., 2004] or for more resources.)

In the case where there is only one teacher responsible for implementing the experimental program, he or she would respond to these questions introspectively.

A CONCLUDING NOTE

An experimental design serves as a framework for conducting the evaluation study. This framework provides an overall conception of procedures to be followed. Being aware of the "big picture" facilitates the work of the evaluation team because its members and other stakeholders whose input they depend on gain an understanding of how the evaluation will proceed. Moreover, describing the way the experimental design was applied should enhance the credibility of the evaluation report since this explanation reflects that a systematic approach was taken in assessing the program.

CHAPTER 4 HIGHLIGHTS

1. Experimental designs are schemes for planning a study. The following designs measure the extent of improvement in program outcomes. The first two involve comparisons of two groups; the third applies to situations with a single group participating. Key features of each design follow:

- **Randomized pretest-posttest control group**
  Randomly assigning students to either the innovative or regular program assumes that both groups are equal (or nearly so) at the start of the experiment. This applies to any student variable that can affect the outcome besides the treatments.
  Pretesting provides a check on whether the groups are initially equivalent on a variable measuring student achievement.
- **Nonrandomized pretest-posttest control group**
  Use this design when it is not feasible to randomize, as in the case of already formed classes.
  Certain extraneous variables are controlled, but it cannot be assumed that both groups are initially equivalent on any student variable that could affect the outcome.
  As in the above design, pretesting provides a check on whether the groups are initially equivalent.
- **One-group time series**
  This design provides a way to determine the consistency of measures before and after the intervention has taken place.
  It does not control extraneous variables as in the previous designs.

2.   Since control of extraneous variables is lacking in a one-group design, it is especially important to substantiate any evidence of noticeable improvement with the judgment of those who have implemented the program.

3.   There may not be students available in the school to serve as a control group; or it may be decided that the program should be open to all those eligible since no one should be denied its potential benefits.

4.   Should there be no control group, a principal may be able to obtain the cooperation of another school similar in student population that would function as this group. However, the use of this school raises logistical issues.

5.   Projecting the findings of the intervention to other students refers to the experiment's external validity.

6.   During the early stages of implementing a modified program a formative evaluation approach should be taken to determine if and how it should be changed. To this end, questions that provide a basis for determining where improvements may be needed were provided for program staff to consider.

7.   An experimental design serves as a framework for conducting an evaluation, thereby facilitating the work of the evaluation team. Describing the design should also enhance the credibility of the evaluation report.

NOTES

1. In discussing random assignment, Fitzpatrick et al. (2004) point out an ethical issue surrounding random assignment whereby only certain individuals are selected to participate in programs offering "great promise" although these have not been tested thoroughly.

2. DuFour and Eaker (1992) maintain that "the renewing school will realize that the quest for continual improvement is never ending" (p. 141).

3. The designs presented in this chapter are based on the work of Campbell and Stanley (1963).

4. Only two pre- and post-measures are shown here. However, if further checks are desired, other testings can be added.

5. These questions are an elaboration of those found in Fitzpatrick et al. (2004) with respect to formative program evaluation. The authors pose the following: What is working? What needs to be improved? How can it be improved?

5

Program Evaluation Through Collaboration

This chapter highlights the formation and operation of a faculty team that relies on collaboration within and outside of its membership to carry out the work of evaluating a program. Given this focus, the following are covered:

- factors for principals to consider in establishing the evaluation team,
- the process for principals to follow in forming an evaluation team,
- guidelines for helping the team function effectively and efficiently,
- preliminary team activities,
- suggestions for the team leader, and
- a partnership with the program staff.

WHY HAVE AN EVALUATION TEAM?

There are several advantages to conducting program evaluation through a team approach:

- collective judgment,
- diverse base of knowledge and skills,

- varied perspectives, and
- shared responsibility.

These are discussed next.

Collective Judgment

In the final analysis, evaluation involves a judgment concerning the effectiveness of a program as well as future directions it should take. These opinions can be enhanced by capitalizing on the collective professional knowledge and insights team members can bring. Consistent with S. Smith (1996), a team represents a critical mass of individuals who can help effect change. Their input, in addition to that of the program staff, provides a source of ideas that should increase the effectiveness and efficiency of delivering a curriculum.

Diverse Base of Knowledge and Skills

Conducting a sound evaluation requires diverse competencies. These include knowledge and skills in the areas of

- leadership,
- management,
- human relations,
- reflective practice,
- data analysis, and
- curriculum.[1]

Furthermore, as a professional development activity, an evaluation project provides a variety of experiences to augment these competencies.

Varied Perspectives

A team composed of faculty members from different grades and/or subjects provides the opportunity for various points of view to surface in judging the worth of a program.[2] This situation can lead to an assessment that is fair and perceived as such. This is not to suggest that only through a team approach can a fair program assessment be made. Certainly, an individual evaluator could do so. However, with a team there is the advantage of determining the effectiveness of a program when different perspectives coalesce in reaching consensus. Thus the judgment of the team members is supported by their dialogue and careful consideration of the evidence to arrive at a common conclusion regarding a program's strengths and also directions for its improvement.[3] Moreover, that this conclusion represents an assessment by peers who understand the conditions and school environment in which the program operates[4] adds to its fairness.

Shared Responsibility

A comprehensive evaluation project requires sufficient time and effort to be completed satisfactorily. While comprehensiveness can help withstand the potential criticism of not having adequate and representative evidence to make judgments, there are simply too many tasks for one or two people to handle in a timely fashion. Thus a team approach makes the effort more manageable.

TEAM COMPOSITION

The team should represent teachers from other grades (or subjects), excluding those staff members implementing the program. This lends credibility to the evaluation report since it would not be written by those who have a vested interest in the program's success. The rationale for this broader representation is not only political: Having faculty with diverse teaching responsibilities participate in an evaluation project facilitates their seeing the interconnectiveness of a particular program in the organizational scheme. This provides a total perspective, which is in keeping with "systems thinking," a characteristic of a learning organization described by Senge (1990), as discussed in Chapter 2. The process of evaluating programs lends itself well to this type of organization.

However, a limitation of a team approach for conducting evaluations could occur any time work is to be done through a committee structure. In this regard, individuals often represent diverse values and ways of doing things. Inherent in a committee's membership is the potential for conflict and differences of opinion for accomplishing tasks. While resolution of differences can produce a better way of doing something, unless a team leader is skilled in the dynamics of group processes,[5] the efforts involved in reaching agreement can lessen the efficiency of team functioning.

Against this background, a principal should try to select evaluation team members, at least for the initial project, on the basis of how well they would work together. Unless this factor is considered, carrying out a program evaluation may be perceived as a negative experience.

FACTORS FOR PRINCIPALS TO CONSIDER IN ESTABLISHING THE EVALUATION TEAM

The prospect of having their programs evaluated is not likely to be eagerly welcomed by many faculty members. A prime reason for this is that teachers, understandably, have a great deal of ego invested in their work. It seems reasonable to assume that they believe they are doing a good job educating students. While they feel they can always improve instruction, they also maintain that they can make a difference in their students. Teachers usually know through personal observation and the "grapevine" which instructors are not very effective and fervently believe that they themselves can do a better job.

Given the egocentric nature of teaching,[6] having programs come under scrutiny could be threatening. Thus it is difficult to separate the quality of a curriculum from those who deliver it. From this perspective, if plans are made to assess their programs, the faculty may perceive that others will associate possible unsatisfactory results with the efforts of those who are responsible for implementing the curriculum. This could generate apprehension. Furthermore, teachers may resist evaluation if they believe that the students' academic levels, attitudes, and behaviors, as well as other conditions of teaching/learning are not conducive to producing successful outcomes.

Faculty may also resist program evaluation if it is regarded as an additional responsibility that would take more time from their busy schedules and add another task to their already heavy workload. This perception is compounded for those staff members who feel stressed and physically tired from what they believe is a difficult teaching situation.

Another obstacle is that teachers are familiar with standardized test results and may not see any further need for determining the worth of a program because they believe that test scores are enough of a measure. Moreover, since teachers are not likely to have had experience with program evaluation, they may not understand its potential for improving educational output.

Any kind of organizational change can be difficult. Staff members are comfortable with routine, and inertia is easier than having to demonstrate new competencies called for by program evaluation. Thus the potential for less than exuberant acceptance of participating in evaluation projects highlights the onus on leadership to promote the value of program assessment to teachers and support their efforts in conducting them. How principals can meet this challenge is discussed next.

FORMING AN EVALUATION TEAM

This section presents guidelines that principals can apply when assembling an evaluation team. They reflect various aspects of the process including promoting, planning, implementing, and supporting the team structure as a regular part of the organization. The guidelines can be communicated by memo and/or at a meeting. Figure 5.1 lists the activities involved in the process; a discussion of each follows.

Figure 5.1 Forming an Evaluation Team: A Guide for Principals

- Communicate the rationale and importance of the evaluation team.
- Emphasize the confirmative and diagnostic functions of evaluation.
- Solicit nominations and volunteers.
- Determine and communicate team size and tenure.
- Decide on the program to be evaluated.
- Announce that a report of the evaluation will be made available.
- Indicate team goals and activities.
- Prepare for questions.
- Emphasize the need for collaboration.
- Describe the responsibilities of the team.
- Describe the qualifications and responsibilities of the team leader.

Communicate the Rationale and Importance of the Evaluation Team

Discuss the rationale for having an evaluation team as an integral and ongoing part of a learning organization. Also explain how the team can disclose information that (a) confirms effective instruction and good student progress, and (b) diagnose conditions to provide direction for improving aspects of teaching and learning.

Emphasize the Confirmative and Diagnostic Functions of Evaluation

Convey that the evaluation team is not a "watchdog" committee whose purpose it is to find deficiencies in a program and its instruction. In contrast, emphasize the importance of the confirmative and diagnostic functions of evaluation.

Solicit Nominations and Volunteers

Encourage faculty to nominate teachers representing various grade levels and/or subjects to serve on the team and also ask for volunteers.[7] Indicate that experience in evaluating programs is a desired, but not a required, qualification for team membership.

Determine and Communicate Team Size and Tenure

The following points should be covered:

- The team will have five to ten members (depending on the size of the school).

- The entire team is composed of faculty members who serve for an academic year with sufficient released time to carry out evaluation activities.[8] Consider the funds available to support released time in deciding on the size of the team.
- If the number of nominees and volunteers exceed the maximum, hold an election. If there are not enough to form a team, a representative group of faculty members should then be asked to serve.
- Secretarial help will be available for typing the report and other material.
- After the year, the team should be composed of new members, except for the previous leader who would now be a member of the new team.
- By continuing in a new capacity, the former leader can share what actions were most effective and efficient as well as the pitfalls to be avoided, thus facilitating the evaluation process.

Decide on the Program to Be Evaluated

In order to help gain faculty support for an assessment project, consensus should be sought on which program to evaluate. However, if you believe that one in particular should be selected, then your reason(s) for recommending or wanting this to be done first should be stated. Doing so can underscore the need for this priority. In any case, sufficient time should be allocated to discuss the issue of which program should receive the focus of the assessment. Providing for this highlights the importance of an evaluation.

Announce that a Report of the Evaluation Will Be Made Available

State that a written report will be disseminated indicating the extent to which a program is accomplishing its goals, what is working well, and which areas may need improvement. In addition, mention that replacing the program could also be a recommendation.

Indicate Team Goals and Activities

A plan for the team's goals and activities should be distributed prior to a meeting so that the staff has the opportunity to discuss its features. Ask the faculty to read it and bring their questions to the meeting.

Prepare for Questions

Anticipate the kinds of questions that might be raised. Consider the potential threat evaluating a program poses as well as other obstacles discussed previously, and think about ways to allay faculty concerns.

Emphasize the Need for Collaboration

To ensure that the evaluation team plan is well received, highlight how the team, in the true spirit of collaboration and professionalism, can be beneficial to faculty members delivering a particular curriculum and, ultimately, to their students' performance.

Describe the Responsibilities of the Team

Team responsibilities include

- meeting with stakeholders (i.e., faculty, administrators, and parents);
- collecting and analyzing data obtained from various sources, for example, students, parents, and those responsible for administering and implementing the program (methods for obtaining data involve surveys, interviews, and collecting student information);
- forming a judgment concerning the effectiveness of the program and offering recommendations for its future; and
- writing a report assessing the evaluation project.

Describe the Qualifications and Responsibilities of the Team Leader

The team leader should be

- an experienced teacher with leadership skills,
- willing to be accountable for the team's progress,
- skilled at conducting meetings,
- task oriented,
- well organized,
- able to mediate conflict and differences of opinion, and
- respected by colleagues.

THE TEAM IN OPERATION

The following guidelines are recommended for helping the team function effectively and efficiently.

The Administrator's Role

At the first meeting with the group, the principal should

- reaffirm his or her commitment to program evaluation;
- stress the importance of the evaluation team;
- remind its members that, since evaluation could be perceived as threatening, they should be sensitive to this and allay any possible concerns of program staff;

- state that he or she is available for consultation and will provide any support that can be given;
- ask the team leader to serve as a liaison between the principal and the team;
- determine a date that would be best for all to hold the first team meeting; and
- indicate that at this meeting a leader will be elected and that all members should review the qualifications for this role.

Preliminary Activities of the Team

At the subsequent meeting of the team, which would not be attended by the principal, the first order of business is to elect a leader and a recorder of the team's activities. The latter position is very important since it requires not only summarizing what transpired at the meetings, but also maintaining a log chronicling the evaluation activities along with completing forms to facilitate carrying them out. The log will be useful in writing the evaluation report.

After electing both individuals, dates for the next meetings should be scheduled. The leader should inform the group that, if necessary, additional meetings may be called. However, these would be held only if needed. The leader should then thank his or her colleagues for their willingness to serve on the team and state that he or she is looking forward to working with them.

Suggestions for the Team Leader

Although Schmoker (1999) advocates effective teamwork for school improvement, he also points out from the works of Little and Katzenbach and Smith, that meetings can be unproductive and unrewarding. According to Katzenbach and Smith, unproductive discussions at meetings can result from lack of disciplined action.

To help ensure that the project is off to a good start, it is recommended that the leader prepare introductory remarks for the first meeting that highlight the need for collaboration in this endeavor. In this regard, Figure 5.2 contains suggested points for orienting the team members to the benefits of a cooperative and synergistic approach for carrying out the evaluation. The leader, of course, may wish to make additions or modifications to these remarks.

Figure 5.2   The First Meeting—Emphasizing Collaboration by the Team
              Leader: Some Suggested Remarks

1. Each of us can make an important contribution to this project.

     There are various interrelated tasks that need to be handled in
     order for the evaluation to be successful.

2. This project involves a team approach in every sense of the word.
   The following are the reasons for this perspective:

     The constraints of time would make it unrealistic for one or two
     people to take major responsibility for conducting the evaluation.

     Our types of experiences and collective professional knowledge
     that we would bring to the team will help ensure the success and
     receptivity of our work.

     In the final analysis we need to reach consensus on determining
     the extent to which the program is effective and provide our
     recommendations for its future. The different points of view
     brought by the team concerning this outcome increases the
     probability of gaining insights that can aid us in forming opinions
     about the program. Thus the consensus we reach should be
     helpful to our colleagues and ultimately, to their students.

   Engaging in the project will enhance our professional development
   in these ways:

     We should gain knowledge about program delivery and
     improvement that is applicable to the curricula we are
     responsible for implementing.

     We will gain competence in assessment approaches that can
     enhance our instructional effectiveness.

   An overview of the evaluation project should be presented next
   (Figure 5.4).

In light of the potential for meetings to become drudgery, "deadly
dull," or indistinguishable from others mired in routine, the guidelines
shown in Figure 5.3 are designed to help team leaders take proactive
steps to help ensure that meetings are events people look forward to attending. Thus meetings should function as a tropism whereby individuals anticipate productive interaction with their colleagues and actually
do gain a sense of professional and personal satisfaction in the process.
Ideal as this prospect sounds, the alternative of not actively seeking this
goal would likely make meetings of an evaluation team be perceived as
"just more work."

Figure 5.3 Conducting Meetings—
Guidelines for the Evaluation Team Leader

- Set the tone for the meetings.
- Ensure that each team member has an opportunity to lend input.
- Send out a meeting agenda.
- Start meetings promptly.
- Be enthusiastic.

Set the Tone for the Meetings

Announce to the group that it is important to feel a sense of accomplishment at the end of each session. For this purpose, allow time near the close of the meeting to summarize what was achieved, and indicate the tasks that need to be completed before the team meets again. The Evaluation Plan and/or Time Log found in Chapter 7 should help the team stay on track.

To facilitate the work of the team, the leader should ask for volunteers to carry out various tasks. If no one offers, the leader will need to assign the particular task. A date for completion should be agreed upon. To minimize the potential for miscommunication, the leader should summarize what needs to be done for each task, unless the activity is obvious. The leader should also write down the person(s) responsible and the due date for each task so that the team member(s) can provide a progress report at a subsequent meeting. This helps ensure that aspects of the project do not "slip through the cracks." Finally, to enhance the continuity and connectiveness of the team's work, state what needs to be covered at the next session.

Ensure that Each Member Has an Opportunity to Lend Input

Explain to the team that its collective knowledge and creativity are best realized when the group engages in the activities of an evaluation project in which all members contribute. Therefore, one or two members should not dominate discussions, nor should anyone be interrupted.

Send Out a Meeting Agenda

The agenda should contain a reasonable number of tasks to complete in the time allocated for each session. At the first meeting, distribute an outline of the program assessment process as delineated in Chapters 7–10. The team leader should be prepared to explain the various tasks involved in carrying out an evaluation study as shown in Figure 5.4.

Figure 5.4 Steps in the Evaluation Process

- Write a program description.
- Formulate evaluation questions.
- Meet with stakeholders to finalize these questions.
- Obtain information to answer the evaluation questions.
- Analyze data to assess the program's impact.
- Evaluate the program's effectiveness and offer recommendations for its future.
- Write the evaluation report.
- Assess the evaluation project.

Start Meetings Promptly

Allow sufficient time, however, for people to get to the meeting place from wherever they are in the building.

Be Enthusiastic

Welcome the members to the first meeting. Also maintain enthusiasm for the evaluation project throughout the entire process.

Extending Collaboration

In line with Fitzpatrick et al. (2004) and Weiss (1998), stakeholders are groups or individuals that have a "stake," that is a strong enough interest in the program's success so that their input should be obtained. However, their participation should not be for political reasons only, but also to provide useful and necessary perspectives as will be evident when the phases of the evaluation project are discussed in Chapters 7 and 8.

An Alliance to Facilitate the Work of the Evaluation Team

Consistent with the site-based evaluation approach taken in this book, collaboration between the evaluation team and other stakeholders involved in and with the school is a dynamic that runs through the entire assessment process. Put another way, the success of an evaluation project hinges on the extent to which the team effectively collaborates with participating faculty members and obtains their cooperation. Along these lines, the input of parents is also essential.

The role that collaboration plays is found in the concept of *participatory evaluation* in which trained evaluators work in partnership with practitioners (Cousins & Earl; Cousins & Whitmore, as cited in Fitzpatrick et al., 2004). While the evaluation team would not be "trained," the notion of being "partners" with the program staff provides a mentality in which determining a program's worth and future would be facilitated. The reason for this is that the effort expended in this judgment is not likely to be hampered by the defensiveness on the part of the program staff that their teaching is at issue. Thus with a partner orientation, the focus is on the program rather than on teacher ability driven by the quest to find or modify a curriculum to complement instruction. To this end, the synergy produced by effective teaching and by an effective program is likely to result in higher student achievement.

A Perspective on the Role of the Principal in the Evaluation Process

While the necessity for collaboration is underscored in carrying out a program evaluation, it is not the responsibility of the principal to micromanage the project. Nonetheless, the principal should be made aware of the team's plans, be kept abreast of its progress, be alerted to any issues and problems that could have organizational implications, and be informed about the need for resources. To depend on the principal to make all decisions, especially those concerning how the project should be carried out, lessens the authority and influence of the team leader and also inhibits the professional growth of the team. Thus the leader, in consultation with the team members, should use his or her discretion regarding the type of input sought from the principal, as well as when administrative approval is necessary for a contemplated action by the team. Giving decision-making responsibility to the evaluators should not be construed as diluting the principal's authority. Ultimately, as the instructional leader accountable for schoolwide programs, the principal has the final decision (if necessary) over those made by the team. The scope of its authority should be stated by the principal when he or she meets with the group at the first orientation meeting. Not informing the team members could lead to resentment if they had the impression that decisions regarding the project were theirs to make and not the province of the administrator.

Role of the Evaluation Team After an Experiment is Planned

Based on its assessment, if the decision made is to experiment with a modified program to determine the effect of the changes, then the team should meet with the faculty participating in the study. This would involve teachers of the experimental and control groups. Procedures for conducting the experiment as well as concepts and principles associated with this type of research would be discussed. (Note that even if a one-group design is used, this meeting should still take place.) Obtaining agreement about plans for carrying out the study should help ensure that a more credible experiment will be conducted.

These plans would include what summative measures should be used to assess the program and a decision on the length of the experimental period. It should end toward the close of the school year to obtain a fairly good idea of the impact the modified program is making. However, shorter programs can, of course, be evaluated sooner.[9]

With respect to characterizing the role of the team in the assessment process, this would be more limited than that carried out when it evaluated the program nonexperimentally. In this regard, the team would still take the responsibility of analyzing student achievement and attitude data, obtaining faculty opinions about the effectiveness of the modified program, and any other information thought to be needed. However, the report should be less formal and comprehensive than that written previously and would contain the extent to which changes were successful and also provide recommendations. The former evaluation team leader would also be available to serve in a consulting role should faculty involved in the experiment have questions.

As a point of clarification, there would be two teams in place at the same time. Having a new team participate in an assessment project helps ensure the benefits to be realized when, in the context of a learning organization, a school provides a mechanism for the ongoing evaluation of its programs. From the perspective of the "previous" team members, determining the extent to which recommendations growing out of their report were successful would likely be seen as a professionally rewarding endeavor. It can therefore serve to put closure on their work.

A CONCLUDING NOTE

As with any project, paying attention to details of an evaluation study increases the potential for its success. When things "slip through the cracks," they detract from the momentum of an endeavor. Time and effort are thereby wasted on trying to fix or complete aspects of an activity that should have been provided for in the first place. This is enervating and frustrating for both the leader of the evaluation team and its members. In contrast, handling details leads to a sense that the leader is thorough which also communicates the importance of the project to the team.

Against this background, the chapter has presented systematic guidelines for the principal and evaluation team leader to follow in the initial phases of the team's operation. For both leaders, these guidelines provide a structure to organize their respective actions, which should therefore facilitate their efforts. When thorough plans for starting and maintaining the work of the team are implemented, these increase the likelihood of enhancing the group's effectiveness and efficiency.

CHAPTER 5 HIGHLIGHTS

1.   There are several advantages of conducting a program evaluation through a team approach:

- Opinions about the effectiveness of a program as well as its future can be enhanced by capitalizing on the collective professional knowledge and insights of the team members.
- Conducting a sound evaluation requires diverse competencies.
- Varied perspectives should result in a fair assessment.
- A team approach makes an evaluation project more manageable.
- Team members representing teachers from other grades and/or subjects, excluding staff members implementing the program, lend credibility to the evaluation report.
- Having faculty from different grade levels (or subjects) serve on the evaluation team facilitates their seeing the interconnectiveness of a particular program in the organizational scheme.

2.   Inherent in a committee's membership is the potential for conflict and differences of opinion. Thus the principal should select team members, at least for initial projects, who work well together. There are several factors for principals to consider in forming an evaluation team:

- Since teachers have a great deal of ego invested in their work, the prospect of having their programs evaluated is not likely to be eagerly welcomed.
- Having programs come under scrutiny could be threatening.
- Faculty may regard program evaluation as an additional responsibility that would take more time from their busy schedules.
- Teachers may not see any further need for determining the worth of a program since standardized test results are enough of a measure.
- Teachers lacking experience with program evaluation may not understand its potential for improving educational output.
- Inertia is easier than having to demonstrate new competencies called for by program evaluation.

3.   Guidelines that principals can apply in assembling an evaluation team cover various aspects of the process including promoting, planning, implementing, and supporting the team structure as a regular part of the organization.

4.   The concept of participatory evaluation by which evaluators work in partnership with the program staff provides a mentality that facilitates determining a program's worth and future.

5.   Suggestions were given for the team leader to help ensure that meetings for carrying out tasks of the evaluation project are productive.

6. The team that evaluated a program still has a role to play when planned modifications are tested experimentally.

NOTES

1. Although not in the context of evaluating programs, the value of a team approach is supported by the research of Katzenbach and Smith (as cited in Schmoker, 1999). They point out that the multiple capabilities of a team are advantageous in dealing with difficult issues.

2. That a team can bring different perspectives in conducting a program evaluation is indicated by the Joint Committee on Standards (1994).

3. A program evaluation should meet the standard of being fair and complete in its assessment by identifying strengths as well as enabling weaknesses to be corrected (Joint Committee on Standards, 1994).

4. The setting and conditions in which a program operates (its context) should be considered in its evaluation (Joint Committee on Standards, 1994). This point is treated in Chapter 8 when areas to cover in drawing conclusions about a program's effectiveness are discussed.

5. Gredler (1996) points out the importance of a moderator having this skill in conducting focus group interviews.

6. Wiggins (1996) believes that "teaching . . . is an egocentric profession in [that] . . . we find it difficult to see when our teaching isn't clear or adequate" (p. 5). However, egocentrism can also have another connotation, one that applies to teachers as well as principals. This involves the conviction that one can be influential in the change process—a belief that underscores the leadership thrust of this book.

7. Initially forming an evaluation committee through volunteers or by appointment is also recommended by DeRoche (1987). He also indicates that eventually committee membership would be elected, appointed, or formed by a combination of these methods.

8. A year is recommended to provide more opportunity for other faculty members to gain experience in evaluating programs.

9. I would like to thank Dr. Andy Henrikson for this useful suggestion.

6

Measuring Program Outcomes

This chapter describes how data collected in various forms are used to measure the impact of programs. The material presented serves as a primer and, as such, is not treated in depth. However, there is sufficient background to facilitate understanding of various dimensions of measurement as these relate to program evaluation.

QUANTITATIVE AND QUALITATIVE DATA

Data can be categorized into two types, quantitative and qualitative. Using numbers for recording and reporting information involves quantitative data. When these data are summarized in some form (e.g., means or percentages), they can be analyzed so that conclusions can be drawn about the worth of a program. Quantitative data are not limited to achievement test scores. They can reflect other outcome variables such as attitudes toward a subject or self-ratings of competencies, perceptions of a program's worth, or behavior.

The other type of data, qualitative, takes the form of verbal information, for example, responses to questions posed during interviews and/or found on survey instruments. Qualitative data provide in-depth descriptions of how situations are perceived. In this way, such data enhance understanding and insights regarding what individuals consider in assessing student growth and the rationale supporting their recommendations for program improvement.

Quantitative data, while less labor intensive to collect and analyze, are no less valuable than qualitative information. Although each type is different, they complement each other (Fitzpatrick et al., 2004), as discussed next.

COMPREHENSIVE EVALUATION

One of the criteria for sound program assessment is that the evaluation should be comprehensive in scope (Joint Committee on Standards, 1994). Essentially, this means that the worth of a program should not be determined solely by one indicator such as a group's performance on a standardized test (Joint Committee on Standards, 1994). The reason for this is that the goals of a curriculum encompass more than what can be measured by a paper-and-pencil test, whether in multiple-choice or essay format.

Obviously, certain outcomes, though worthy in their own right, cannot be assessed by achievement tests—standardized or otherwise. Examples of such outcomes include the success of community service projects, attitudes toward a subject, the quality of student interaction with teachers and other students, and the confidence level shown when displaying knowledge in classroom situations.

Data from these types of indicators can be measured by colleagues observing a teacher's lesson; others can be tapped by having students complete self-rating scales. However, outcomes can also be assessed by eliciting opinions expressed in the form of qualitative data, which may corroborate measures obtained quantitatively. Thus while faculty judgment of student progress stated in qualitative terms is more subjective and impressionistic because it is not obtained directly from respondents, as in the case of an attitude instrument,[1] opinions are nonetheless important evidence to have. They contribute to the comprehensiveness of the evaluation and also provide a more "human touch" to assessment information (e.g., asking a teacher to explain her favorable reactions to a program). By obtaining illustrations to support this position, evidence becomes more concrete. Thus readers can relate to and/or understand information more readily, thereby extending the meaning of results reported in numerical terms.

Teacher opinions also add an important dimension to evaluation data because they are based on professional judgment. In this regard, because teachers assess their students formally and informally, they are in the best position to ascertain if any improvement in achievement, attitude, or behavior can be linked to the learning activities of a program being examined. They can make this judgment because it is grounded in their experience with other curricula and students similar to those who are (or who have participated) in the current program.

Obtaining opinions is not limited to faculty. Those given by others, for example, parents, the administrator(s), or the coordinator, as well as students, provide additional perspectives and therefore broaden the base of evaluation data. In sum, the type of qualitative data described here provides one of the valid determinants of program effectiveness.

VALIDITY AND RELIABILITY OF EVALUATION DATA

This section describes two criteria to apply in judging the accuracy of information obtained in conducting an evaluation—validity and reliability.[2] Meeting the validity criterion involves determining whether the information disclosed by the data collection procedure contributes relevant evidence regarding the outcome assessed.[3] To ascertain the reliability of the procedure, the information it provides is examined for its consistency. Each of these criteria is discussed next.

Validity

Collecting Valid Data—Some Issues to Consider

Obtaining valid evaluation data is crucial to the perceived worth of the evaluation report. This is particularly true for those delivering and administering or coordinating the program. They need to feel that the judgment of the team was based on solid evidence and that its report reflects a fair assessment. This belief makes it more likely that the report will be accepted and its recommendations put into practice.

It is not easy to accept criticism about one's work, even if it is couched in the form of positive recommendations. When teachers believe that they have provided good instruction but learn that certain changes are called for in the program, it is difficult to separate their own involvement with aspects of the curriculum and related processes that need remediation. The possibility of defensiveness, coupled with the feeling that routine is often more comfortable than change, can make recommendations for program improvement difficult to accept. This is especially so when an evaluation is based on information that individuals most directly affected by an assessment do not find creditable. This underscores the need for obtaining evaluation data believed to be valid by those whose reputation and work are affected by an assessment of their programs.

Consequently, leaders should be sensitive to the personal or human side of program evaluation, which extends beyond the technical dimension.[4] If faculty concerns are neglected or given short shrift, this could generate resistance to the entire evaluation project and minimize cooperation—an indispensable factor in conducting an assessment study. The actions discussed in the next section should help avoid the negative fallout associated with data considered not to be fair, useful, or accurate.

Collecting Valid Data—The Process

The evaluation team should invite faculty teaching in the program to a meeting to elicit their input concerning the types of assessment data needed and the plan for obtaining this information. If the program has a coordinator, this person would, of course, also be involved in the data-planning phase of the evaluation project. The program staff should participate with the team in its deliberations regarding the type of data to be collected since the conclusions and recommendations of the team can affect the way teachers conduct their classes in the future. Thus the team has an ethical obligation to seek the professional perspectives and ideas of those delivering the program. Not only is this the right thing to do, but it is also politically expedient because it would likely lessen objections or resistance to decisions thought to be made unilaterally (i.e., without involvement of those directly responsible for implementing the curriculum). Regarding what the team and program staff should consider in collecting summative data in the form of test results, guidelines are indicated in Figure 6.1.

Figure 6.1   Data Collection Issues to Discuss Between the Evaluation Team and Program Faculty

---

- Determine if the latest standardized test results are recent enough to be included as part of the pool of evaluation data. If they are outdated, consider administering a standardized test that is aligned with one or more goals of the program.

- Similarly, the results of textbook tests may be available (or could be given) if the data from these would meet the alignment criterion stated above. This information should also be used as evidence regarding the program's effectiveness.

- If the faculty of the program believes that what they have taught can best be assessed by a teacher-made instrument, then its use should be encouraged. For this, a summative type test should be developed, if one is not already available. This instrument should contain a representative sample of items that reflect student knowledge, understanding, and abilities and serve as one of the overall measures of their growth over a certain period of time.

- If the aim was to develop higher cognitive abilities and/or creativity in the form of, for example, written expression or problem solving, these types of outcomes should be tapped.

The Role of Faculty in the Program Not Being Evaluated

If two programs are being compared, it is important that teachers from both reach consensus on which test(s) and assignments will be used to determine the worth of the curriculum being assessed. This would provide balance in the evaluation process and thereby, help ensure fairness of the findings.

To facilitate obtaining agreement between the faculty in each program on the test(s) to be used, teachers in the pilot program should first resolve this issue. Then the selection, stated in tentative terms, should be presented to the staff members implementing the regular curriculum to determine if this is acceptable to them. This can be done at a meeting conducted by the team of faculty from both programs or by memo. Further negotiations on this matter may be necessary. With consensus reached concerning the type of actual test(s) that will provide evidence of the pilot program's effectiveness, teachers from both programs can work together in constructing or selecting the instrument(s).

Judging the Relevancy of Tests

As with any data collection procedure, a test should first be assessed to determine if the data it provides would be a suitable indicator of a program's outcome or operation. One approach for making this assessment is to judge the content of the test according to whether its items include a representative sample of tasks that require students to demonstrate what they have learned consistent with the goals of the program. If the test meets this criterion, it can be characterized as having content validity since it yields information that allows one to draw reasonable conclusions about the program's effectiveness. Guidelines for judging the content validity of a test by those teaching the program are given in Figure 6.2. If more than one teacher is involved, then consensus on each of these issues must be reached.

Note that the guidelines can also enhance future performance on mandated, standardized tests since the questions raised call attention to what actions are needed to prepare students for these tests.

Figure 6.2 Judging Content Validity of a Test—Guidelines for Teachers

- Based on prior performance on periodic tests given during the year, do most students have the knowledge and skills to answer the item correctly?

- Do students have adequate experience with the type of task posed by the item?

- Have teachers covered the material sufficiently for most students to be able to answer the item correctly?

- Overall, do the items reflect the degree of emphasis they received during instruction? For example, if teaching focused equally on math computation and solving word problems, then the test should be divided about equally between each of these competencies.

Responding to the questions posed in the guidelines for determining content validity of nonstandardized tests can be facilitated by using the form shown in Figure 6.3. The form is divided into two parts. The first involves assessing each item. For the second part, a comparison is made between the estimated percentage of instructional time allocated to a particular knowledge or skill area and the percentage of items on the test that cover that area. Based on this comparison, adjustments in the number of items that relate to a topic can be made accordingly.

Figure 6.3   Determining Test Validity

Part A
Individual items

Item Number	Material covered sufficiently (✔ if "yes")	Most students should be able to answer this item correctly (✔ if "yes")	Students have had experience with this type of task (✔ if "yes")	Decision about item: Retain Modify Reject

Part B
Entire test

Knowledge or skill area	Estimated percentage of instructional time	Percentage of items covered on the test

A Further Note on Test Validity

Judging a test for content validity enhances the accuracy of the evaluation since an instrument would be used that has adequately represented the material taught. Thus a fairer assessment of the program's impact can be made because students have a better opportunity to demonstrate their achievement. Moreover, there should be less frustration and better morale on the part of students as well as teachers since there is likely to be more success with tests that yield valid data.

Reliability

Earlier it was stated that reliability of evaluation information refers to its consistency. Reliability is an essential criterion when considering the use of a data collection procedure since evidence must be dependable if it is to be accurate.

Judging Test Reliability

One way of determining whether a test provides consistent results is to check, on an item-by-item basis, what percentage of students in the top quarter of the group that took the test answered each question *incorrectly*. If this proportion is relatively large (i.e., over one-third), then this indicates less consistency in performance. When this occurs for more than 10 percent of the items (although, admittedly, this is an arbitrary margin of error), reliability is questionable.

If an item meets the "over one-third of the group" criterion, consider it a candidate for modification before inclusion in another test. Two parts of the item—the problem and the answers—should be checked. For multiple choice instruments, keep a tally of the option that was most often chosen incorrectly. If a pattern is clear, then compare this option to the right answer and reword it so that it is more distinct from the correct response. When one wrong answer is not predominant, the problem portion of the question may need to be clarified. Teachers should review this situation to determine whether the item ought to be revised or discarded. If any part of the item is modified, the revised version can be stored as part of a test bank for future use.

Additional Checks on Test Reliability

A nontechnical approach to measuring reliability is to examine the *internal consistency* of responses to a test by comparing the mean scores obtained on the odd and even numbered items. If these scores are fairly close, it can be assumed that the results are consistent. This can be verified further by comparing the percentages of odd and even items answered correctly.

The following points will help guide this process of determining reliability:

- If the entire test contains an odd number of items, both of the preceding approaches can be used since means and percentages are involved.
- Determining if the reliability measures under discussion are close is a judgment call that should be decided by consensus of the team and teachers in the innovative (or pilot) and regular programs.
- Using means and percentages, the test performance of students participating in the program being evaluated can be compared with those in the regular program. As indicated previously, this is done

by taking the total scores earned by each student on the odd and even sets of questions. However, the means and percentages of each set are calculated *separately for each group* since students in one program may have achieved higher. Therefore, the extent to which the results differ within each group would indicate if the performance of students in their respective programs was consistent. If there is only one group involved in the evaluation, then the internal reliability of what the instrument yields can still be checked.

The following are other approaches for determining if the results of a test are reliable. A *test-retest* procedure can be applied. This involves administering the same test a short time later (e.g., two weeks) and the overall means of the students in *each* program can be compared to measure how closely the averages are. (The same procedure is applicable if only one program is involved in the assessment.) Note that if the interval between testings is too short, students may supply the same answers on the retest based on what they remembered from first test. This is in contrast to demonstrating the knowledge or skills called for by the items. Conversely, if the time between tests is too long, the learning of new material may better prepare students to answer the retest simply because they have had more time to gain familiarity with the material. This situation can make the results less consistent.

If enough items exist to assemble another test or if a similar instrument that measures the same abilities is available, then the method of *equivalent forms* (or *alternative forms*) reliability can be applied to determine the extent to which students' performance is consistent. This approach eliminates the issue of students possibly responding based on remembering their previous answers. The similar test can be given very soon after the first one. In fairness to students, if there is a difference in scores for any individual, the higher one should be used.

It should be noted that not all of the procedures to determine consistency of results need be used. The constraints of time dictate how many will be applied. The decision on this issue should be made by consensus of teachers in the program(s). However, using only one method would still provide a practical indicator of reliability.

To determine how consistent scores are on tests and assignments that are not objectively graded, separate assessments of the work from each class by two teachers from the same grade level (or department) can be compared. Mean scores are also used for this analysis. With this approach, the extent of *interscorer reliability* (also referred to as *interrater reliability*) would be determined. The use of agreed-upon rubrics would help ensure that grading is done according to a common standard.[5] Moreover, the value of measuring the extent of agreement on assessing students should be discussed between the evaluation team and the teachers in both programs. In this regard, what should be conveyed by the team is that interscorer reliability can enhance the objectivity of assessment evidence and thereby contribute to the credibility of the evaluation's findings.

A further consideration in determining reliability is that situations out-side of the test itself can affect the reliability of results. Thus an instrument could be well constructed in that its directions and items are clearly stated. However, due to an interruption or other distractions, students' concen-tration may have been adversely affected. It could also be that not all of the teachers followed directions in administering the test the same way. Such situations can lessen the consistency of results.

Communicating Techniques for Determining Test Validity and Reliability

When test results are both valid and reliable, this supports these findings as indicators of program effectiveness. Thus outside of one that is mandated, a test should be screened against the criteria of validity and reliability.

Meeting these criteria enhances the fairness of the evaluation process. The reason for this is that the students' demonstration of knowledge and skills tapped by a test may be handicapped by inappropriate or faulty items. Along these lines, the teachers' efforts and the potential of the program itself may not be fully realized by such inadequacies of the instrument.

Given this possibility, it would be worthwhile if the evaluation team shared validity and reliability techniques with the teachers in both pro-grams being compared. Knowledge of this type is consistent with the pro-fessional development thrust of a learning organization. Thus as faculty learn about and practice assessment techniques, this should have the cor-responding effect of producing a more sound evaluation.

To facilitate teachers' abilities in the areas of test validity and reliabil-ity, time needs to be allocated for such training. Here is where the leader-ship of the principal is essential in promoting and supporting the staffs' acquisition of assessment knowledge. This disposition can be demon-strated by including the topic of test validity and reliability during a day devoted to professional development. Covering these aspects would ex-pand the knowledge base for faculty members whose programs are not the focus of the evaluation, but who would benefit from this exposure when they construct or modify tests. Having teachers from different grade levels (or subject areas) gain knowledge about techniques for enhancing validity and reliability is consistent with "systems thinking," one of the disciplines of a learning organization that is advocated for schools (Senge et al. 2000).

In support of the need for teachers to gain competency in determining if tests accurately measure student achievement, Stiggins (2004) argues that "teachers must possess and be ready to apply knowledge of sound classroom assessment practices" (p. 26). He takes his position to this level: "If teachers assess accurately and use the results effectively, then students prosper. If they do it poorly, student learning suffers" (p. 26). He would prevent the negative consequences of inadequate assessment knowledge by his remedy of offering "targeted, productive professional develop-ment to put the available classroom assessment wisdom into the hands of practitioners" (p. 26).

While Stiggins (2004) refers to evidence of student learning gathered by teachers each day as influencing "the most crucial instructional decisions" (p. 26), his perspective is certainly relevant in terms of analyzing evaluation results to judge the quality of an entire program. This is especially the case since a curriculum provides an overarching structure that defines the type of teaching and learning activities pursued. Therefore, its effectiveness can, in fact, have a marked impact on everyday "crucial instructional decisions."

A Further Note on Reliability

Determining if information is reliable is not limited to one procedure. In this regard, there should be consistency among the types of evidence analyzed that were collected by various methods (e.g., observations, interviews, or questionnaires) in order to draw conclusions about the impact of a program. However, it should also be pointed out that, for certain outcomes, a trend in responses indicating overall support of the program among different groups may not be present. Of course, differences of opinion could occur. Where these differences are found, they do not suggest that a particular tool for collecting evidence has yielded unreliable data.

PERSPECTIVES ON AUTHENTIC ASSESSMENT

In summarizing points made by several writers, Gredler (1996) states three expectations for authentic assessments: "(1) . . . they should guide reform by focusing classroom effort toward more intellectual tasks, (2) . . . be more meaningful to students because they indicate real-world challenges, and (3) . . . influence the professional development of teachers" (p. 134).

Authentic assessment typically involves performance assessment and portfolios (Gredler, 1996). The former, according to Haertel (as cited in Gredler), "requires examinees to demonstrate their capabilities by creating some product or engaging in some activity" (p. 129). More specifically, the behavior or product assessed "is valued in its own right outside of the test setting" (Gredler, p. 129). Examples of learning activities involving performance assessment given by Gredler include experiments, essays, and research projects.

With respect to portfolios, according to Gredler (1996), their use in program evaluation is problematic at best because of the difficulty involved in "providing standardized reporting of student accomplishments across classrooms, schools, and perhaps, districts" (p. 161).[6] As another approach to authentic assessment other than portfolios, Gredler calls attention to the use of rubrics in assessing student achievement. In this regard, as found in Costa and Kallick (1995), rubrics can involve such indicators as critical thinking skills if such outcomes are sought by the curriculum being evaluated. In this effort, the need for collaboration within and across programs being compared is underscored to determine which tests (or items) and assignments will be used to measure student progress that is not assessed by traditional grading.

Evaluating Curricular Processes

For individuals to improve in any endeavor, it is necessary to assess their overall performance. Such assessment identifies the area(s) that need to be "worked on" in order to do better the next time. Even though proud of a particular accomplishment, high achievers from various arenas intuitively grasp which aspects of what they have done still need to be strengthened. This sensitivity and focus, plus feedback from others, contributes to what makes them excel.

In this same vein, the *process* dimension of conducting an evaluation study provides information for areas that need improvement. Taking specific actions is crucial here since performance efforts must be efficient; this requires focus. When actions are focused, by definition, they are concentrated. In this regard, physical and mental energy are channeled into a synergistic force to facilitate the achievement of a particular goal.

This mentality is applicable to improving test performance whether on an authentic or a standardized instrument. With a focused orientation, an inquiry needs to be made regarding factors that affect how the curriculum is being delivered. The means for obtaining this type of formative information is discussed in Chapter 7.

The Place of Improvement in Program Evaluation

Although school performance is judged in summative terms by end-of-year testing, what is inherent in the learning process and guides the work of teachers is grounded in the degree to which students show improvement. In this regard, by reviewing test scores, grading assignments, and making regular observations, teachers are aware of the progress of their class and plan instruction accordingly including what to emphasize. In this context, a "fringe benefit" of teaching is the gratification of seeing students make gains.

While they may have to be made aware that they are doing better compared to when they were first learning something, students have an intuitive sense of whether they are making progress. This sense of growth is potent. It works its way into the fabric of attitudes held by students about what they are learning. As such, levels of attitude and motivation are inextricable. Thus measuring the extent of improvement goes to the heart of the educational process and is therefore a worthwhile indicator of program effectiveness in its own right. From this perspective, improvement should be an important consideration in judging a curriculum's worth along with summative outcomes that compare its participants with other students. As a brief preview of Chapter 8, it contains practical applications on how various indicators of improvement can be analyzed.

A CONCLUDING NOTE

If assessing a program consisted solely of measuring student achievement by standardized testing, there would be no need for an evaluation team. The worth of a program would be determined on the basis of students' performance as reflected in grade-equivalent scores or state-mandated criteria. However, evaluation is more than measurement. Assessing a program is a multidimensional endeavor that, in the final analysis, involves the exercise of professional judgment. Such judgment is expressed in opinions regarding the intervention's effectiveness as well as recommendations for improving the program or for its termination. These opinions rely, in part, on the knowledge of basic measurement concepts and awareness of assessment issues covered in this chapter.

If students' work is performance based, then correspondingly, achievement should be authentically assessed. When the evaluation team seeks information that reveals the extent to which traditional and authentic assessment support the program's effectiveness, the comprehensiveness of the evaluation is enhanced. Consequently, conclusions drawn about the curriculum are more definitive because corroborative rather than narrowly based evidence has been obtained.

CHAPTER 6 HIGHLIGHTS

1. Data can be categorized into two types, both of which should be collected in an evaluation study:

- **Quantitative** uses numbers.
- **Qualitative** involves verbal information.

2. An evaluation should be comprehensive, that is, a number of outcomes should be used to determine the worth of a program.

3. Evaluation data should meet the criteria of

- **validity**, which involves determining whether the information disclosed by a data collection procedure contributes relevant evidence regarding the outcome assessed; and
- **reliability**, which ascertains whether the information provided by the procedure is consistent.

4. In order to collect valid information, the evaluation team should elicit input from the staff delivering the program regarding the types of assessment data needed and the plan for obtaining these.

5. Guidelines for judging the content validity of a test involve the items themselves as well as other factors relating to students and teachers.

6.   Determining content validity enhances professional development because it is a reflective activity.

7.   Reliability is an essential criterion in considering the use of a data collection procedure since evidence must be dependable (i.e., consistent) if it is to be accurate.

8.   One way of determining whether a test provides consistent results is to check, on an item-by-item basis, what percentage of students in the top quarter of the group that took the test answered each question incorrectly.

9.   There should be consistency among the types of evidence analyzed that was collected by various methods.

10. Other methods for judging the reliability of test results involve measuring the consistency of

- odd and even items answered correctly,
- performance on a test and retest and between equivalent forms, and
- teacher agreement in scoring student achievement.

11. It would be a worthwhile professional development activity for teachers to gain competency in techniques for determining test validity and reliability.

12. The process dimension of conducting an evaluation study provides information for areas that need improvement.

13. The extent of improvement should be an important consideration in judging a curriculum's worth along with summative outcomes that compare its participants with other students.

NOTES

1. As used in this book, an instrument is broadly defined to include any tool employed for obtaining data, e.g., tests, questionnaires, or observation scales.

2. These criteria are two of those that comprise the Accuracy standard in *The Program Evaluation Standards* (Joint Committee on Standards, 1994).

3. Based on *The Program Evaluation Standards* (Joint Committee on Standards, 1994), a data collection procedure could consist of, for example, tests, questionnaires, observations, interviews, and student records.

4. In this vein, Posavac and Carey (2007) discuss the importance of the technical as well as the interpersonal skills of evaluators.

5. The application of rubrics in performance assessment is discussed by Gredler (1996) and examples are given for different subjects. In this process, establishing interrater reliability by involving faculty is discussed by Gredler (1996).

She separately cites authors (Archbald & Newmann; Mitchell) in reporting how teams of teachers first agree on writing standards and then papers are scored by two readers.

   6. In her book on program evaluation, Gredler (1996) devotes an entire chapter to portfolios as an alternative measure of performance assessment.

7

The Evaluation Process: Phases 1, 2, and 3

T his chapter provides the structure for obtaining comprehensive information in assessing the factors involved in delivering a program, as well as its outcomes. Following the systematic approach[1] as presented enhances an evaluation project's credibility. To this end, a variety of data sources is used to judge a program's effectiveness and efficiency.

An evaluation study begins by selecting an established program to assess, that is, one that has usually been functioning for at least a year.[2] It can be a regular part of the curriculum or one that is ancillary (e.g., a pull-out or afterschool program).

The reason that a program should be usually evaluated after a minimum of one year is to provide an opportunity for it to make enough of an impact so that a sound judgment can be made regarding its worth.[3]

In this chapter, the first three stages of conducting an evaluation are covered:

- Phase 1—Describing the program
- Phase 2—Providing direction for the evaluation
- Phase 3—Obtaining information to answer evaluation questions

PHASE 1—DESCRIBING THE PROGRAM

In this phase, a description of the program to be evaluated is written. For this task, members of the evaluation team interview program staff to obtain needed information and also refer to any document available describing the program. This is a crucial step because a sound evaluation depends on how much those judging the program know about its goals and operation. Furthermore, faculty in a program being assessed should believe that the evaluation team really knows what the teachers are trying to accomplish and how they are going about it. This adds to the perception of a fair evaluation.

The areas to be covered for writing the description are outlined next.[4] A discussion of each follows.

- Overview of the Program
- Program Goals and Objectives
- Program Operation
     Selection of participants
     Characteristics of participants
     Instructional activities
     Program personnel
     Management activities
     Material resources
     Schedule
     Costs

Overview of the Program

This section provides an orientation regarding the type and nature of the curriculum. The information given would be in more detail than that reflected in the title. Describe the following aspects of the program:

- type and nature of the program, for example, regular, remedial, honors (note that the nature of the program would be reflected in its title that is stated in the heading for the program description);
- population served (i.e., whether it is designed for all students at one or more grade levels or only for those with special needs);
- who developed the program (e.g., textbook publisher, central office curriculum department, teachers at a local school who made adaptations of an existing program);
- how long it has been in operation;
- where it is being offered—districtwide, one or more schools; and
- other information that helps orient the reader to the nature and scope of the program.

If the program represents a special initiative (e.g., a pilot program), then the need for it should be indicated. In such instances, describe the problem or situation that provided the impetus for developing the program. If it is not a special program, change the title of this section to "Introduction." Then state that it is part of the regular course of study and specify the grade level(s) involved.

Program Goals and Objectives

These are presented in the form of a list. Note that objectives are more specific and are more easily measured than goals. An example of an objective would be to raise grade-equivalent reading scores at least one year for sixth-grade students who are one or more years below grade level.

In contrast, a goal may simply state to improve reading achievement of sixth-grade students.

If objectives were not originally formulated, then these would not be included in the description. However, if the goals do not already exist in a document, then those responsible for delivering the program need to be surveyed to determine this information.

Program Operation

This part describes the structure of the program, other aspects that characterize it, and the resources that enable it to function. More specifically, the program's operation is delineated by addressing the following.

Selection of Participants

Indicate how students were chosen and what criteria were used in this process. Also specify the number of students the program served. If all students at a particular grade level are involved (e.g., a reading or math curriculum for grades four, five, and six) this should be noted.

Characteristics of Participants

In general terms, describe the nature of the students who are in the program, for example, above average or at risk.

Instructional Activities

Highlight the key features of how the program is being (or was) delivered with respect to both teaching and learning approaches.

Program Personnel

Specify the number of people who are (or who were) involved in implementing the program and their respective roles (e.g., four teachers, one of whom served as the coordinator). Include any use of volunteers such as parents or other community members.

Management Activities

Describe the role of the program coordinator or administrator. Specify the major responsibilities involved.

Material Resources

Describe the use of any equipment or learning material in more detail than that indicated under the instructional activities section.

Schedule

State how often each class meets and the length of each session.

Costs

Provide information regarding total costs including that expended for personnel, equipment, and material. If the program is part of the curriculum, only indicate any special costs, funds allocated for expenses beyond textbooks, or learning materials that are regularly furnished to students by the school.

Further Aspects of Phase 1

Based on the description of the program, a reader should have a good idea of its purpose(s) and operation. The description also provides background for developing and selecting *evaluation questions*. The information disclosed from answering these will be used to judge the effectiveness and efficiency of the program. Thus these questions provide direction for the evaluation study (Fitzpatrick, Sanders, & Worthen et al., 2004).

As indicated previously, another benefit of writing a clear description is that it demonstrates to the program staff that the evaluation team is very familiar with the curriculum under assessment. If staff members perceive that the team is knowledgeable in this regard, they are more likely to be receptive to the evaluation report since it would be seen as being based on informed judgment.

When the description has been written, it should be presented to those responsible for implementing the curriculum to obtain feedback on its accuracy. Any corrections should be made and the description resubmitted to the program's personnel.

PHASE 2—PROVIDING DIRECTION FOR THE EVALUATION

It was stated earlier that the evaluation procedures described in this book focus on processes for delivering a program and student outcomes. To obtain information on both of these dimensions, *evaluation questions* are used to guide subsequent phases of the project. Thus these questions help the evaluation team think about the kinds of data needed to answer them, the methods to be used for collecting and analyzing such data, and also form a basis for drawing conclusions about the program's methodology and impact. Furthermore, a set of evaluation questions serves as a framework that facilitates organizing the report of the study.

The following steps are involved in carrying out Phase 2:

- Formulate evaluation questions
- Present the evaluation questions to stakeholders
- Generate other possible evaluation questions
- Assess outcome questions
- Obtain consensus between stakeholders and the evaluation team on the final choice of questions to be used

Formulate Evaluation Questions

Evaluation questions are designed to obtain information about the outcomes of the program and related processes used to achieve those outcomes. Questions that concern outcomes should be stated so that they flow easily from each goal. Thus if it was the intent of the program to elevate reading achievement and also increase interest in reading, then these or similarly phrased questions can be used:

- Has the afterschool reading program been effective in raising reading achievement?
- Has interest in reading increased as a result of the program?

A question should also be raised concerning outcomes that may have occurred but which were not originally intended such as:

- Were there positive outcomes that occurred that were not indicated in the goal statements?

According to Weiss (1998), evaluators should be aware of unanticipated consequences of a program (i.e., results not intended) that are positive as well as negative. Outcomes that may be negative can be identified by eliciting information about how the program can be improved, which is covered by a later question. Opinions given in this regard can serve the dual purpose of disclosing areas of deficiency in the program's operation and also provide potential remedies for improvement.

The following can be placed under the umbrella of a process question that is apropos for the staff teaching in the program:

- Are there features of the program that were especially useful in helping students learn?

This question identifies particular strengths of instructional delivery. Such information can be used when plans are made to modify the program, thereby helping to ensure that what has been found to work will continue. In this regard, Weiss (1998) maintains that the quality of particular program features and activities and the way they are delivered will affect the extent to which outcomes are successful.

In addition to determining the extent to which a program has been successful in achieving its outcomes—the effectiveness dimension of evaluation—another criterion to investigate is the curriculum's efficiency. This aspect concerns judging if the outcomes produced were worth what they cost (Weiss, 1998). An economic perspective on worth is appropriate here because efficiency concerns the issue of whether resources expended to operate the program were put to best use, that is, were well spent. With this in mind, the following evaluation question adds another dimension to the assessment process by tapping opinions of program staff and the administrator(s):

- Are the outcomes produced by the program worth the time and/or money expended to prepare for and implement it?

The information that would be obtained by this question is not, by itself, typically used to judge program efficiency. What is commonly carried out for this purpose is, according to Weiss (1998), a technical approach that is usually in the form of cost-benefit and cost-effectiveness analyses.[5] This situation notwithstanding, an evaluation question eliciting opinions about resources used, while subjective and not expressed in economic or accounting terms, is nonetheless useful. The reason for this is that such opinions are grounded in the professional experience of those who deliver or are responsible for administering the program. Thus if the weight of evidence indicates that resources were well spent, this reinforces the value of the program. In contrast, if information reveals that financial and/or time expenditures were too high relative to program outcomes, then such information could (a) serve as a stimulus for thinking about how resources can be better spent or (b) lead to the adoption of a more promising program.

Next is a generic evaluation question concerning curriculum processes:

- Are there recommendations for improving the program or its delivery?[6]

How this question can be extended to obtain specific suggestions to strengthen the program will be described in Phase 3.

The following is the final evaluation question to ask:

- Should the program continue in its present form, be modified, or be replaced with one that appears more promising?

This is a summative question[7] that focuses on judging the program's effectiveness in overall terms. When posed as an interview question, responses can further disclose how strongly people feel about their position. Thus answers that are elaborated upon contribute perspectives that should be useful when the team presents evidence to confirm its recommendations concerning the future of the program.[8]

More About Evaluation Questions

The language for these questions can be the same (or similar to) that used for interviews or found on questionnaires which require a written answer. For example, the evaluation question "are there recommendations for improving the program or its delivery?" can be modified to "do you have any recommendations for improving the program or its delivery?"

How survey questions are phrased and for whom they would be appropriate depend on the group involved. Since open-ended questions provide the opportunity to obtain more in-depth information, respondents should be asked to explain their opinions.

In sum, the set of evaluation questions discussed reflects two types, those that relate to the program goals and those that are generic in that they are applicable across different curriculums being evaluated. Regarding the latter, there are advantages to having a standard set of generic questions. For one, it lessens the opportunity for disagreement over which items to use when these are presented to individuals outside of the team. It is also more efficient in terms of saving time in writing and selecting potential questions. In support of this point, those that are generic are designed to tap opinions that cover various perspectives concerning a program's outcomes and how it functions. Thus the data elicited by answering goal-related and generic questions would tend to be comprehensive and therefore, not narrowly focused. To this end, it is recommended that all five generic items be incorporated in the evaluation along with the others. Moreover, having the same set of generic issues to address provides a standardized approach for assessing other programs. This can be useful in demonstrating accountability by communicating how the school is continuously seeking ways to improve its curriculums.

Present the Evaluation Questions to Stakeholders

After the goal-related questions have been written by the team, these, along with the generic items should be distributed at a meeting attended by the program staff, the principal, and other stakeholders (nonschool personnel). This will provide a forum to explain the purposes of both types of questions.[9] The reason for this step is to foster an understanding of how the information obtained by addressing evaluation questions enables a judgment to be made about the program's effectiveness and efficiency.

Thus when stakeholders are made aware of the importance and function of each question, this would enhance understanding of what is involved in conducting a comprehensive evaluation. Figure 7.1 summarizes the rationale for the two types of questions and should facilitate explaining the orientation of each. (Chapter 8 indicates sources that provide information to address these questions and how the data obtained from these sources can be analyzed.)

Generate Other Possible Evaluation Questions

Next, ask stakeholders if they have suggestions for other questions. Indicate that these should be formulated to evaluate the overall effectiveness of the program. Put another way, the questions should help determine if the program is successful thus far (or was successful). For this purpose, also inform stakeholders that their questions should aim at measuring results or *outcomes* in light of the program's goals.

To guide the writing of outcome questions, apprise stakeholders of the following criteria:

- Considering the goals of the program, is the question suitable?
- How feasible is it to answer this question given the availability of (a) the information sources and (b) time?[10]

Outcome questions should be edited to eliminate any duplicates. If time permits, they would be discussed at the same meeting or at one subsequently scheduled as described next.

Assess Outcome Questions

In this step, the stakeholders and the team judge which goal-related questions should be addressed by the evaluation study based on the two previously stated criteria—their suitability and feasibility. This determination should yield a more manageable set of questions to investigate.

Obtain Consensus Between Stakeholders and the Evaluation Team on the Final Choice of Questions to Be Used

The intent of this step is to help ensure that the different stakeholder groups involved are in accord regarding how the types of information elicited by the set of questions can provide for a comprehensive evaluation since a variety of perspectives will be brought to bear on judging the program.

It is especially important that there be understanding between the team and the program staff as to what will finally be asked. In this regard, for Fitzpatrick et al. (2004), agreeing on evaluation questions by consensus results in a "feeling of 'shared ownership' which greatly enhances the probability that evaluation findings will be used" (p. 250). Moreover, if parents representing the larger group of stakeholders are "on-board" with the outcome

Figure 7.1 Categories of Evaluation Questions

Question	Type	Function	Purpose of Information Obtained
1. Has the afterschool reading program been effective in raising reading achievement? *	Goal related	Outcome (Summative)	Contributes evidence of programs effectiveness (i.e., impact or success). Provides input concerning decisions about continuing the program (Fitzpatrick et al., 2004).
2. Has interest in reading increased as a result of the program? *	Goal related	Outcome (Summative)	Same as above.
3. Were there positive outcomes that occurred that were not indicated in the statement of goals?	Generic	Outcome (Summative)	Same as above.
4. Are there features of the program that were especially useful in helping students learn?	Generic	Process (Formative)	Identifies particular strengths of instructional delivery.
5. Are the outcomes produced by the program worth the time and/or money expended to prepare for and implement it?	Generic	Outcome (Summative)	Provides evidence of program's overall efficiency.
6. Are there recommendations for improving the program or its delivery?	Generic	Process (Formative)	Indicates specific direction for either modifying the program or remediating deficiencies in its delivery.
7. Should the program continue in its present form, be modified, or be replaced with one that appears more promising?	Generic	Outcome (Summative)	Provides input to help judge overall program effectiveness.

*This question is an example and would thus be modified to reflect the program's goals.

and generic questions, this puts them in a better position to support the evaluation. In turn, when their involvement and advocacy of the project is communicated to other parents, this lends credibility to the undertaking.

Organizing Assessment Results

Evaluation questions facilitate the systematic arrangement of evidence concerning various aspects of a program's operation and outcomes. Functioning this way, these questions help the evaluation team present a "case" to support its judgment about the worth of a program. To this end, results germane to a particular question are subsumed under it. The process involves a decision by the team regarding what information provided by which group(s) involved can best address the issue being raised. Thus depending on their content, results from items excerpted from surveys in written or oral form can also be placed under a certain evaluation question if the findings contribute information to answer it. In other situations, it would be appropriate to use an entire instrument, for example, if it tapped student attitudes toward a subject and the question raised also focused on this variable as a program goal. In sum, any data, no matter how collected, can provide evidence relevant to a specific evaluation question.

Gathering such evidence is facilitated when strategies for this task are in place. Team members can then systematically direct efforts more efficiently because they know what specific information to look for and how to go about finding it. The *evaluation plan* shown later in this chapter provides a road map for guiding Phase 3 of the project.

PHASE 3—OBTAINING INFORMATION TO ANSWER EVALUATION QUESTIONS

After the evaluation questions have been agreed upon, the process of collecting evaluation information is ready to begin.

Preliminary Considerations

Determine if a control group is available to serve as a basis of comparison to judge the program being assessed. (Refer to Chapter 4 to review the different approaches for obtaining a control group.) If a comparable group is not being used, baseline data (e.g., pretest measures such as test results and report card grades) are needed to judge the extent of improvement.

The question of whether to use a sample or the entire population should be resolved. The following speaks to *not* using a sample:

- If only a relatively small number of individuals are involved, then using a sample is unnecessary (Fitzpatrick et al., 2004; Weiss, 1998). For example, collecting information from two to four classrooms would not be too time-consuming.

- Since the school has results of standardized tests, this information may be readily available if the evaluation plan calls for such information.
- If an additional nonstandardized test is being administered as an outcome measure to determine program effectiveness, teachers would have the scores from this test anyway. The evaluation team could divide the task for summarizing these data (e.g., by calculating means and percentages) based on the performance of all students. The same holds true for report card information.

Using a Sample

The prime reason for sampling is that the resources available to the team in terms of personnel and time may be limited if the data from the entire population were to be collected and analyzed. Given this possibility, the team has to estimate what is feasible to accomplish. Therefore, a sample size that is manageable needs to be determined. For this purpose, the guidelines in Figure 7.2 should be helpful.[11]

The numbers in this figure are based on drawing a sample from a single population. However, if program participants and nonparticipants are being compared, then appropriately sized samples should be drawn from each of these populations.

Figure 7.2 Population Size and Required Sample Size

Population	Sample
300	180
400	208
500	230
600	246

After the sample size has been determined, an expedient way of obtaining the sample is to select classes (rather than individuals) so that their total enrollment is at least that of the size desired. The process for choosing samples in this way is called *cluster sampling* where each group, in this case a class, is known as a cluster. The following are steps for choosing sample classes.

1. Number each class on separate slips of paper, fold, place in a container, and mix the contents.

2. Draw one slip, note the class number, and replace the paper in the container. The reason for replacing the slip is to keep the probability of selecting a sample constant (i.e., drawing one class out of the *same* total number of classes each time).

3. If the same group is drawn again, it is ignored since it was already chosen. Replace the slip and pick another.

A Note on Selecting Classes Randomly

If students are enrolled in a special program being assessed (e.g., one offered after school), then selecting entire classes may not initially provide the required sample size. The reason for this is that both participants and nonparticipants may be attending the same classes in which a survey will be distributed. Therefore, it would be necessary to have a place on a questionnaire that asks students to designate whether or not they were participants. If the sample size is not obtained after the first administration of a questionnaire, then a second set of classes can be randomly selected shortly afterward to make up for the deficit in sample sizes.

A further point: When only a sample of classes is chosen to participate, even randomly, the assessment of the program may be criticized by teachers and parents as being neither fair nor accurate since input was not obtained from all classes. More specifically, consider the situation where the program was judged as only moderately successful. However, assume classes that had performed relatively well were excluded from the sample. Their teachers may feel that the report does not represent the students' performance.

While it would be more political to include input from all classes, there is, nevertheless, a reality to consider when conducting focus (small) group interviews with students. If these were to involve a fairly large group, say two hundred (or even more), then such interviews may take too much time and thereby delay issuing the evaluation report. In this regard, the evaluation project should not be overly ambitious. If this occurs, the work could become onerous, rather than productive. Therefore, using a smaller group may be more feasible. How to obtain a sample for these interviews is discussed later.

With respect to parents, it is good public relations to inform them of program changes. When improvements are planned, they would like to know that their input was considered. Sending questionnaires to the entire population provides this opportunity as well as broadening the base of support.[12]

In sum, when all members of different stakeholder groups have the chance to contribute evaluation data, this enhances ownership in the revised program. Another issue is that after doing all of the work required for an assessment project, the evaluation team should not be in the position of finding that their work is unnecessarily criticized. This could have an adverse effect on its morale as well as dampen the spirit of the succeeding team.

Selecting Focus Groups

One approach for deciding on the sample size to use in conducting focus group interviews is to have the evaluation team decide on how many of these are practical to schedule. For example, the decision might be to hold twenty interviews, each involving a group of five students—ten group interviews for the innovative and ten group interviews for the regular program (fifty students from each set). Assume that the population of each program is approximately 150 students. Two separate lists are composed, one containing names from the innovative program and the other from the regular group. Since the sample size is one-third of 150, then every third name is selected from each list until there are 50 students representing each program.

Selecting respondents in this way is known as *systematic sampling*. While this method is not random sampling because everyone did not have an equal chance of being selected, systematic sampling should produce a representative sample more efficiently than by drawing names from a container. Systematic sampling, can, of course, be used if there is no control group.

Note that although it is important to plan data collection procedures, the team may find that after it has begun conducting focus group interviews, there is time to use this method to obtain information from every student.

With respect to teachers, all who have taught in either the innovative or regular program should be surveyed. First, there is greater opportunity to obtain a diversity of opinions, both favorable and unfavorable. Second, it is more political to have greater inclusiveness. Also, not involving everyone could lessen the report's credibility because some teachers who were not surveyed could feel that their opinions did not count. Moreover, having a greater number of opinions, including input from administrators and coordinators, provides the opportunity to obtain more reliable evidence because one can better determine if there is consistency among the responses.

Data Collection Methods

Methods for collecting data should be selected to address each of the evaluation questions. This requires tapping a variety of information sources using multiple procedures (e.g., test scores, questionnaires, and interviews) in order for the evaluation to be comprehensive (Joint Committee on Standards, 1994). When this criteria is met, there is greater opportunity for the results to be consistent which would thereby strengthen conclusions drawn about the program. Discussed next are various factors to consider and suggested actions to take with different approaches to collecting data.

Obtaining Opinions from Stakeholder Groups

An important dimension of a program evaluation is the measurement of opinions. This involves examining the positions of stakeholders who have different levels of knowledge and involvement concerning how a curriculum is being implemented, its goals, and what has actually been accomplished. Thus consistent with Borg (as cited in Brainard, 1996), the opinions of teachers as input for evaluating a program, while subjective, should be weighted heavily. Subjectivity notwithstanding, their judgment adds a professional perspective to assessment data that contributes to the comprehensiveness of the evaluation. In this regard, teachers have been involved with the mechanics of a particular curriculum enough to know firsthand if it facilitates their instructional efforts or whether other learning material is necessary because a program was not working very well.

Concerning the opinions of parents, their input can corroborate that of the staff. Thus how their child reacts to and engages in a subject outside of a classroom learning environment helps crystallize parental judgment about a program's quality.

Obtaining Information on What Students Believe

When a program's goal is to improve student attitudes, instruments for measuring this outcome may be available in the school or district. If no questionnaire is found that suits this purpose, then an online search can be made using the descriptor: student attitudes toward (fill in the subject).

Using a search engine should disclose a questionnaire consistent with the goals of the program that can be used in its entirety, be shortened, or be modified by changing or combining items from different instruments. If, however, the team in consultation with the program staff feels that developing its own questionnaire may be more suitable for the attitudes the program has sought (or is seeking) to foster, then an instrument can be developed for the evaluation study. Examples of attitude items are given later in this chapter. Keep in mind that unless otherwise indicated, permission should be obtained to use or change a copyrighted instrument.

Items that are written for a new questionnaire would cover such aspects as the extent to which students

- feel that the material is interesting or difficult,
- enjoyed assignments or classroom activities,
- felt confident about learning and taking tests,
- were motivated to learn, and
- perceived that they were improving or were mastering course content.

Note that certain items developed for a student questionnaire can also be reworded to elicit opinions from parents concerning indicators that reflect their child's attitudes, behaviors, motivation, difficulty in learning, confidence, and progress about a particular subject. Moreover, the instrument need not be long in order to obtain this assessment.

Prior to developing an instrument, the responses of students given during focus group interviews can be phrased as items that tap perceptions. Further, while the questionnaire does not have to be relatively long, it does take time to assemble one that measures various dimensions of attitudes. Therefore, it is recommended that the team make an initial search for an instrument that already exists that can be used as is or modified.

Connecting Interviews and Questionnaires

As a method of inquiry, interviews enable one to gain additional insights about the effects of the program. This is likely to occur because of the opportunity interviews provide for obtaining in-depth responses.

As indicated earlier, interview questions can also be the same as (or similar to) those used for the evaluation questions. This is also the case for open-ended items on a survey questionnaire. No matter how the data collection procedure elicits information from respondents, the language should be phrased so that it is appropriate to the perspectives of different stakeholder groups.

For example, the following evaluation question can also be used to obtain information from interviews conducted individually or in focus groups with program staff in which the respondent is asked to support his or her answer:

Has interest in reading increased as a result of the afterschool reading program?

- Please explain.

On a survey questionnaire sent to parents, the question can be phrased as a statement to record the degree of agreement with the issue raised as measured by a *Likert scale*, as illustrated under the following examples:

My child's interest in reading has increased because he or she has been in the afterschool reading program.

Strongly agree	Agree	Undecided	Disagree	Strongly disagree

For a survey completed by students, the statement might be phrased as:

I like to read more because I have been in the afterschool reading program.

Depending on the age of the students, the same scale previously shown for the "parents' question" can be used. Another possibility is the following:

Agree very much	Agree	Not sure	Disagree	Disagree very much

When constructing or using an instrument, the number and type of response categories to use on a scale should be determined by the evaluation team in consultation with the program staff. To be decided is whether students have the cognitive maturity to make the judgments called for by the gradations of the scale. Thus for older students a five-option format could be appropriate. For those who are younger, a shorter scale should be used as the one shown next:

Yes   Not sure   No

For interviews with students concerning, for example, interest in reading, they could be asked this question:

Do you like to read more because you have been in the afterschool reading program? Why? (Why not?)

Interviewing Parents

As previously discussed, interviews can be held using small focus groups (e.g., four to five students). With parents, interviews can be conducted by phone if it is more expedient to do so. Selecting parents to interview can be done by the systematic sampling method described earlier. The sample size would depend on the amount of time the evaluation team can devote to this activity.

An Advantage of Interviewing

This method provides more of an opportunity for the interviewer to obtain in-depth information by asking the respondent, representing any group, to explain an answer or elaborate on it and/or to give an example or two.

The rationale for conducting interviews is to gain more insight into how an individual feels about the issue raised than is possible when an option is selected on a Likert scale or when only a brief written response is given to an open-ended question. Thus understanding an individual's position enables the evaluation team to make any judgment and recommendation in a more informed way.

A Further Perspective on Conducting Interviews

Concerning the use of interviews in an evaluation study, writers (Fitzpatrick et al., 2004; Posavac & Carey, 2007; Weiss, 1998) indicate the need for the interviewer to establish rapport with the respondent. In this regard, Weiss maintains that the better the relationship, the more likely is the respondent "to give full and accurate answers" (p. 167).

While greater disclosure is more probable in a relationship built on trust,[13] rapport should not require special effort if the purposes of the evaluation were framed in terms of a partnership between the evaluators and program staff at the onset of the project. With this perspective, the principal and team leader, in discussing the benefits of evaluation with the program staff, would point out that the intent of the project is not to judge teaching competence. Instead, what should be communicated is that with collaboration and cooperation of the staff, the team would gather evidence to determine which aspects of the curriculum are particularly effective, which areas need improvement, and whether the program should be replaced with an alternative that could better aid instruction.

With the stage set by the leadership of the principal and evaluation team leader for a collaborative approach to evaluation, it would be worthwhile if the interviewer reiterated the partnership theme at the beginning of the session. This sets the tone for the interview process making it conducive for obtaining more complete information since the respondent, consistent with Posavac and Carey (2007), should be less guarded when answering. This atmosphere facilitates greater reflection on the part of the interviewee. In sum, a partnership mentality is aligned with the tenets of a learning organization that continually seeks to identify what actions are effective in helping achieve its goals and what needs to be improved, a point worth noting when discussing the value of program evaluation with the faculty.

Follow-Up Questions

If students who participated in the intervention are now in a higher grade, or if they were in an ancillary program such as one offered after school, then the current teacher(s) in the same school should be asked follow-up questions. Answers to these provide additional information on program outcomes, thereby disclosing evidence regarding how *durable* the effects of the intervention are with respect to students who are no longer participants. An example of a follow-up question is shown next:

> Are these students, as compared to others you now have (or have had), achieving particularly well, and if "yes," in which way?

Data can also be obtained from these teachers regarding other indicators of program effectiveness (e.g., interest in reading). These types of questions would be formulated based on the goals of the program. However, a generic question should be raised, such as the following:

> Have you observed anything special about these students concerning the way they perform or do their work as compared to others?

The answers may reveal a positive outcome that was not the intent of the program, for example, a higher level of self-confidence.

The information obtained from each follow-up question should be subsumed as evidence under its appropriate evaluation question.

Obtaining Formative Information

Recall that one of the evaluation questions asks if there are recommendations for improving the program or its delivery. This information, from the perspective of those implementing the program, can be obtained through a needs assessment as shown in Figure 7.3. The instrument is comprehensive; it covers issues of curricular content, instructional activities (processes), and learning materials. Opinions are also elicited involving a variety of factors that can affect how well the program functions and consequently, student outcomes. The formative information yielded by the instrument should result in more efficient efforts directed at improving the program because time, energy, and resources can be concentrated on areas of greater need.

Figure 7.3 Program Needs Assessment

Name of Program:_____

Directions

Listed below are items regarding a variety of factors that can have an impact on the effectiveness of the program being evaluated.

- For each item, please indicate the extent of need for change by checking the box.
- Indicate any recommendation(s) that could improve delivery of the program or its operation.

| | | Extent of need for change: | | | |
		None needed	Low priority	Medium priority	High priority
1.	Inservices for teachers* Recommendation(s) for improvement:	❑	❑	❑	❑
2.	Curriculum is aligned with standards.* Recommendation(s) for improvement:	❑	❑	❑	❑
3.	Scheduling of the program Recommendation(s) for improvement:	❑	❑	❑	❑
4,	Changing the textbook Recommendation(s) for improvement:	❑	❑	❑	❑
5.	Modifying or adding other learning materials* Recommendation(s) for improvement:	❑	❑	❑	❑
6.	Instructional methods Recommendation(s) for improvement:	❑	❑	❑	❑
7.	Changing the curricular content* Recommendation(s) for improvement:	❑	❑	❑	❑

Figure 7.3   (continued)

| | Extent of need for change: | | | |
	None needed	Low priority	Medium priority	High priority
8. Changing the sequence of curricular content*	❑	❑	❑	❑

Recommendation(s) for improvement:

_____

_____

9. New content makes connection to prior material taught.	❑	❑	❑	❑

Recommendation(s) for improvement:

_____

_____

10. Assignments provide for sufficient opportunity to apply material taught.*	❑	❑	❑	❑

Recommendation(s) for improvement:

_____

_____

11. Assignments provide for regular practice.*	❑	❑	❑	❑

Recommendation(s) for improvement:

_____

_____

12. Learning activities reinforce teacher instruction effectively.	❑	❑	❑	❑

Recommendation(s) for improvement:

_____

_____

13. Assignments regularly provide for review of material.*	❑	❑	❑	❑

Recommendation(s) for improvement:

_____

_____

14. Learning activities are motivating. *	❑	❑	❑	❑

Recommendation(s) for improvement:

_____

_____

15. Classroom assignments keep students actively engaged in the learning process.	❑	❑	❑	❑

Recommendation(s) for improvement:

_____

_____

Figure 7.3   (continued)

	Extent of need for change:			
	None needed	Low priority	Medium priority	High priority
16. Eligibility of students for participation in the program**	❏	❏	❏	❏
Recommendation(s) for improvement:				
17. Teachers need to meet more frequently to discuss and/or collaborate on articulation (i.e., continuity of learning activities across grade levels) and other curriculum issues as well as instruction.*	❏	❏	❏	❏
Recommendation(s) for improvement:				
18. Productiveness of these teacher meetings with respect to the discussions and/or collaborative efforts*	❏	❏	❏	❏
Recommendation(s) for improvement:				
19. Based on regular testing, follow-up is geared toward the specific area(s) of deficiency.	❏	❏	❏	❏
Recommendation(s) for improvement:				
20. Learning activities are suitable for students with different ability levels.*	❏	❏	❏	❏
Recommendation(s) for improvement:				
21. Students have received training on how to respond to questions posed on different types of exam formats (e.g., multiple choice).	❏	❏	❏	❏
Recommendation(s) for improvement:				

Figure 7.3 (continued)

| | Extent of need for change: | | | |
	None needed	Low priority	Medium priority	High priority
22. Students understand what a question is asking and therefore know how to supply the correct answer.	❏	❏	❏	❏

Recommendation(s) for improvement:

_____

_____

| 23. Students realize the need to read a test item carefully in order to know what a question calls for. | ❏ | ❏ | ❏ | ❏ |

Recommendation(s) for improvement:

_____

_____

| 24. Students understand the vocabulary found in various types of questions and/or assignments that have special meaning for a particular subject. | ❏ | ❏ | ❏ | ❏ |

Recommendation(s) for improvement:

_____

_____

| 25. Students have experience in taking "practice" standardized tests. | ❏ | ❏ | ❏ | ❏ |

Recommendation(s) for improvement:

_____

_____

| 26. Students' explanations regarding how they solved the problem or why they gave an answer to a question has provided insight to guide subsequent instruction. | ❏ | ❏ | ❏ | ❏ |

Recommendation(s) for improvement:

_____

_____

| 27. Students have a solid foundation in the basics of a subject.* | ❏ | ❏ | ❏ | ❏ |

Recommendation(s) for improvement:

_____

_____

Figure 7.3   (continued)

	Extent of need for change:			
	None needed	Low priority	Medium priority	High priority
28. Students have sufficient knowledge, understanding, and skills to learn more advanced subject matter.	❏	❏	❏	❏
Recommendation(s) for improvement:				
29. Students complete all or most homework assignments at a satisfactory level.	❏	❏	❏	❏
Recommendation(s) for improvement:				
30. Students have experienced being successful on tests and assignments on a regular basis.*	❏	❏	❏	❏
Recommendation(s) for improvement:				
31. Students feel confident that they can obtain good or even excellent test scores and grades.	❏	❏	❏	❏
Recommendation(s) for improvement:				
32. Students are able to learn more challenging material.	❏	❏	❏	❏
Recommendation(s) for improvement:				
33. Learning activities provide for the development of higher problem solving abilities.*	❏	❏	❏	❏
Recommendation(s) for improvement:				
34. Students' attitudes are positive.	❏	❏	❏	❏
Recommendation(s) for improvement:				

Figure 7.3 (continued)

| | Extent of need for change: | | | |
	None needed	Low priority	Medium priority	High priority
35. Efforts are directed at soliciting support and involvement of parents with program activities.*** Recommendation(s) for improvement:	❏	❏	❏	❏
36. Are there any other aspects of the program that need attention? Please specify level of priority. Recommendation(s) for improvement:	❏	❏	❏	❏

---

* Items 1, 2, 7, 8, 10, 11, 13, 14, 17, 18, 20, 27, 30, and 33 are based on material indicated by DeRoche (1987) concerning various aspects of a curriculum or text.
** This item would apply to ancillary or other programs that are distinct from the regular curriculum (e.g., an afterschool or honors program).
*** This item is based on an indicator of effective schools reported in reviews by Purkey and Smith (1983 and 1985) as cited in DeRoche (1987).

Responses to this questionnaire may disclose deficiencies that are external to the curriculum, which can nevertheless limit its effectiveness. In this regard, the program may not be realizing its potential to produce desired outcomes. If this is the case, corrective actions can be taken as would be indicated in the evaluation report. After an agreed-upon period of time, teachers can then meet to determine if students are making better progress. This approach gives the program a "fair" chance to demonstrate its worth and frees the faculty from seeking to fix something that may be inherently sound to begin with.

With respect to improving an aspect of the program's operation, the respondents are asked to indicate the extent of need for change. Also requested are any recommendations for improvement. After the results are tabulated, focus group interviews with the program staff can be scheduled concerning recommendations that require elaboration or further clarification. The interviews should target those suggestions where a trend in the data is evident for "medium- and high-priority" items.

A Note About Interviews

Focus group or individual interviews with program staff should also be conducted to address the other evaluation questions. The decision to use either method or a combination of these for any of the questions depends on the time available to the team as well as the program staff. It may be necessary to schedule more than one session.

Figure 7.4   Procedures for Conducting Classroom Observations

Conduct classroom observations at consistent times.

Visits should take place during the same time period (i.e., a session in the morning or afternoon) and within a certain time frame (e.g., two weeks).

Use more than one observer.

This lends reliability to the measurement.

Carry out a series of observations.

Sufficient data are needed in order to draw more reliable conclusions about classroom activities. If only one observation is made, a class may have had either an "off" day or a particularly productive one. Thus it is recommended that two to three observations be conducted.

Observe a control group.

If available, a control group should also be observed to provide a basis of comparison.

Conducting Observations

Another evaluation method involves classroom observations. The procedures recommended for conducting these are given in Figure 7.4.

Carrying out observations can provide useful information since evaluators then have another source of tangible evidence concerning the program's effectiveness. However, teachers may resist the prospect of peers coming into their classrooms to assess the extent of learning taking place. Thus they may not feel comfortable with observations because these can easily be construed as "Not only is my program being evaluated, but so is my teaching." Consequently, permission for having the evaluation team members visit classrooms should be obtained before any observations are made.

Given the possibility of a negative reaction to observations, the principal should reassure the teachers that they are not being evaluated as individuals. In this regard, he or she should communicate that all professionals can improve through feedback, and that the delivery of a program can be enhanced in this way as well. In efforts to allay possible concerns, teachers should be reminded that a sound program evaluation also confirms learning activities that are effective.

A rating scale such as the one shown in Figure 7.5 can be used to record observations. The list of items is not meant to be exhaustive and can be modified to suit specific situations. Moreover, this type of instrument can serve the dual role of eliciting program processes and outcome data. Comments given in the space provided below each item can provide a source of information for making recommendations to improve the program.

Figure 7.5   Classroom Rating Scale

Date:_____

Observer:_____

Goal(s) of the lesson observed:

1._____

2._____

Students are participants in the program being evaluated.* ____Yes ____No

1.   Students were actively engaged in the learning process.

| 1 | 2 | 3 | 4 | 5 | NA (not applicable) |
Low   High

Comment:

_____

_____

2.   Students responded well to the teacher's questions.

| 1 | 2 | 3 | 4 | 5 | NA |
Low   High

Comment:

_____

_____

3.   Students raised "how" and "why" questions.

| 1 | 2 | 3 | 4 | 5 | NA |
Low   High

Comment:

_____

_____

4.   Students were attentive when the teacher gave explanations.

| 1 | 2 | 3 | 4 | 5 | NA |
Low   High

Comment:

_____

_____

5.   Students appeared well prepared for the lesson.

| 1 | 2 | 3 | 4 | 5 | NA |
Low   High

Comment:

_____

_____

Figure 7.5   (continued)

6. Students displayed appropriate classroom behavior.

	2	3	4	5	NA
Low				High	

Comment:
_____
_____

7. Students appeared to be interested in the lesson.

	2	3	4	5	NA
Low				High	

Comment:
_____
_____

8. Students used their time productively.

	2	3	4	5	NA
Low				High	

Comment:
_____
_____

9. Students responding to the teacher's questions was not limited to a few individuals.

	2	3	4	5	NA
Low				High	

Comment:
_____
_____

10. Students demonstrated understanding of the lesson by their responses.

	2	3	4	5	NA
Low				High	

Comment:
_____
_____

11. Students held an effective dialogue with the teacher.

	2	3	4	5	NA
Low				High	

Comment:
_____
_____

Figure 7.5   (continued)

12. Students held an effective dialogue with each other.

    | 1 | 2 | 3 | 4 | 5 | NA |

    Low   High

    Comment:

    _____

    _____

13. Students made appropriate references to the text.

    | 1 | 2 | 3 | 4 | 5 | NA |

    Low   High

    Comment:

    _____

    _____

14. Students were able to use learning material besides the text
    effectively.

    | 1 | 2 | 3 | 4 | 5 | NA |

    Low   High

    Comment:

    _____

    _____

*This information is included when an innovative program is being compared to a regular one.

Organizing Procedures for the Evaluation Project

Before collecting any type of information, plan for this activity by reading Chapter 8, which discusses various types of data analyses. Then complete the Evaluation Plan, a model of which is shown in Figure 7.6. (Note that the space below each item can be expanded to accommodate more information if necessary.) The plan (including copies of interview questions and survey questionnaires) should be presented to the principal, program staff, and other stakeholders to obtain feedback and consensus.[14]

Figure 7.6 Evaluation Plan

1. Evaluation question:

    _____

    _____

2. Information requirements (What information is needed to answer the question?):

    _____

    _____

3. Information source (Where and how can the information be obtained?):

    _____

    _____

4. Instrument(s) or measurement(s) used:

    _____

    _____

5. Design (Indicate comparisons to be made, e.g., comparing two groups on a test or pre- to posttest gains for one group.):

    _____

    _____

6. Schedule for obtaining data (Set date[s] for collecting this information.):

    _____

    _____

7. Data analysis (How will results be summarized to help answer the question?):

    _____

    _____

From _Program Evaluation Skills for Busy Administrators_ by T. R. Owens. © 1979 Northwest Regional Educational Laboratory. Adapted with permission.

Agreement on the plan is essential. Thus in order for an evaluation report to have influence on the decisions about the future of a program, it must be perceived as credible. In this regard, it is crucial that interpretations of data be accepted by stakeholders (Posavac & Carey, 2007). Such acceptance would be made easier when, as writers have advocated, there is agreement on the criteria to be used in assessing a program (see, e.g., Fitzpatrick et al., 2004; Posavac & Carey, 2007).

Schedule project activities by completing column 1 of the Evaluation Time Log (Figure 7.7). As each activity is finished, enter the date in column 2. This should facilitate planning the team's work since one would be able to see the extent to which the deadlines set have been met.

Figure 7.7 Evaluation Time Log

	Completion Date Set	Date Activity Completed
1. Determine the scope of the evaluation.		
a. Write the program description.	_____	_____
b. Formulate the first set of evaluation questions.	_____	_____
c. Agree with stakeholders on final set of evaluation questions.	_____	_____
2. Plan the evaluation.		
a. Complete parts 1–4 of the Evaluation Plan.	_____	_____
b. Complete parts 5–7 of the plan.	_____	_____
3. Implement the evaluation.		
a. Administer instruments as scheduled in the plan.	_____	_____
b. Collect other data.	_____	_____
c. Analyze data.	_____	_____
4. Report the evaluation study.		
a. Submit draft copy to stakeholders.	_____	_____
b. Submit final report.	_____	_____

From *Program Evaluation Skills for Busy Administrators* by T. R. Owens. © 1979 Northwest Regional Educational Laboratory. Adapted with permission.

Ethical Aspects of Program Evaluation

In assessing the worth of a program, evaluators face several ethical issues. Among those that Weiss (1998) discusses is the need to maintain confidentiality and anonymity of all information obtained in an evaluation. Aligned with Weiss' point, when information is not identified as having come from a specific source, this has implications for building trust and cooperation not only for the current evaluation study but for future projects as well. Thus individuals should not feel threatened or reluctant to provide evaluation data for fear that their program may be assessed as less than satisfactory. Such an assessment could be perceived by the program staff as lowering their status among members of the school community. People should therefore feel free to express their opinions (Weiss, 1998) in the context of providing accurate information that can improve program delivery. Consistent with Weiss, such freedom can occur when those interviewed believe that by giving their opinions of a program, they will not be identified by name in the evaluation report or informally by the evaluation team to administrators and other faculty members.

In the case where there is only one faculty member providing instruction in the program being evaluated (e.g., an honors class), then maintaining confidentiality and anonymity, is, of course, not possible. However, if the evaluation report is to be disseminated beyond the district, it is best that the teacher's name not be indicated unless permission is given to do so.[15] A further point is that if the environment of the school truly reflects a learning organization, then a teacher should not be concerned about expressing his or her opinions since such input could be useful in improving the program. Such freedom is an outgrowth of a principal's leadership in promoting and supporting professional and student growth through experimentation with innovative and promising curricular changes.

Another ethical issue that Weiss (1998) discusses is informed consent. This means that the evaluation team must respect the rights of individuals who do not wish to provide information on any aspect of the program. Along these lines, the team must adhere to the policy of the district with respect to obtaining parental permission for students to give input concerning their experiences with an innovative or regular program as well as other student data.

Guidelines for Collecting Evaluation Data

This section synthesizes the approach to data collection procedures discussed in this chapter and also covers other aspects to consider when carrying out these procedures.

1. If an evaluation study involves a comparison between two programs or if only a single program is being assessed, the same set of evaluation questions is used.

2. With a two-group design, separate interview questions should be formulated so that they are applicable to each program respectively. For example, the staff teaching in the innovative program could be asked the following:

How effective is the innovative program in raising math scores?

| Very effective | Effective | Somewhat effective | Not very effective |

For instructors in the regular program, the same type of question and scale is posed. However, the word "regular" is substituted for "innovative". The next question is apropos to those currently teaching in both programs:

As compared to the regular curriculum, how effective is the innovative program in raising math scores?

Very   Effective Somewhat Not very   Equally   Neither is
effective   effective effective effective effective

Note that the scale accompanying the interview questions should facilitate making a judgment by the respondent. The reason for this is that a continuum provides a frame of reference that clarifies the relative choices available. Another advantage of using such a scale is that it makes it easier to analyze and report responses. For example, a report might present this finding:

> Three out of four teachers in the innovative program believed it to be very effective in raising math scores. One felt it was only somewhat effective.

Whether or not a scale is used in conjunction with interview questions, respondents should be asked to explain their answers. Such explanations provide further evidence to support the opinions given.

3. When comparing two programs, the items on a survey questionnaire should be generic so that they apply to both. As previously stated, the Likert scale on which the respondent records his or her answers should be appropriate for the person's age. Note the applicability to both programs in these examples:

> What I am learning in my English class helps me in my other subjects.
>
> Strongly   Agree   Not sure   Disagree   Strongly
> agree   disagree
>
> It's easy for me to learn new things in math.
>
> Yes   Not sure   No
>
> I like the discussions we have in my social studies class.
>
> Strongly   Agree   Not sure   Disagree   Strongly
> agree   disagree
>
> My science class is interesting.
>
> All of the   Most of   Sometimes   Never
> time   the time

Generic items on a survey questionnaire (as well as interview questions appropriate for each group) provide a current basis of comparison. In this regard, the responses of students in the innovative program are examined against those given by participants in the regular curriculum.

For a one-group design, interview questions and survey questionnaire items, would, of course, refer only to the intervention. Examples are given next.

This question can be posed to the staff:

> To what extent has the innovative program been effective in raising math scores?

Very effective	Effective	Somewhat effective	Not very effective

A questionnaire item for students can be stated in this way:

> I can read better because I have been in the afterschool reading program.

Yes	Not sure	No

Note that all of the survey questionnaire items shown have been stated positively. These can be phrased as such if the instrument is relatively short. However, if a longer questionnaire is constructed (or adapted), then the possibility of *response set* is increased. This refers to the tendency of an individual to answer a certain way, for example, strongly agree (or agree) throughout the questionnaire. Interspersing some negatively stated items on the instrument could lessen this tendency. These items would be, with the most positive response receiving the highest number of points as shown in the next example using a five-option Likert scale.

My science class is boring.

	Strongly agree	Agree	Not sure	Disagree	Strongly disagree
Points assigned	1	2	3	4	5

The next item elicits the same opinion, but it is stated positively with the points indicated for each response.

My science class is interesting.

	Strongly agree	Agree	Not sure	Disagree	Strongly disagree
Points assigned	1	2	3	4	5

Whether the item is stated positively or negatively, the middle option on a five-point scale is still worth three points.

4. Both quantitative and qualitative data should be obtained whenever it is possible to do so. Having both types serves to corroborate conclusions drawn about a program's effectiveness.

CHAPTER 7 HIGHLIGHTS

1. The following constitute the first three phases of program evaluation:

- Describing the program
- Providing direction for the evaluation
- Obtaining information to answer evaluation questions

2. Describing the program is a crucial first step since a sound evaluation depends upon how knowledgeable those judging the program are about its goals and operation.

3. Evaluation questions accepted by stakeholders through consensus are designed to obtain information on program processes and outcomes. These questions provide direction for subsequent phases of the assessment project.

4. Various data collection procedures should be used for a comprehensive evaluation.

5. An evaluation plan and an evaluation time log serve to organize the work of the team.

6. Interviewers should establish rapport with the respondent by reiterating the partnership theme of evaluators and program staff.

7. Consistent with ethical aspects of program evaluation, the team must maintain confidentiality and anonymity as well as obtain informed consent regarding the participation of individuals in the evaluation study.

NOTES

1. The evaluation process presented in Chapters 7 and 8 is based on the approach found in the works of Fitzpatrick et al. (2004) and Owens (1979).

2. In the case where a program is not scheduled throughout the year (e.g., a new summer school initiative), a decision would need to be made about when a summative evaluation should be conducted. To resolve this issue, consider when there would be enough evidence accumulated to address the evaluation questions discussed in this chapter. In this regard, the decision involves determining after how many times the program has been implemented it is thought ready to be evaluated.

3. In discussing when to evaluate programs, Fitzpatrick et al. (2004) caution that too-early summative judgments may result in scuttling programs which, with fine-tuning, may have turned out to be successful. In this regard, the authors quote Campbell who recommends waiting a year or so during which debugging would occur before evaluating a program.

4. The program description headings have been modified from Owens (1979).

5. See, for example, Fitzpatrick et al. (2004), Posavac and Carey (2007), Weiss (1998) regarding methods of determining program costs. There are a number of

points made by Weiss (1998) in her discussion of analyses for determining program efficiency that are pertinent to this evaluation question. These include the factor of time as a cost, the need for judgment, and having information concerning decisions about future options for a program.

6. If the program has been completed, ask how it could be improved should the decision be made to continue it in the future as in the case of submitting a proposal for refunding.

7. This question is consistent with the aspect of summative evaluation that, according to the Joint Committee on Standards (1994), involves recommendations about whether a program "should be retained, altered, or eliminated" (p. 209).

8. The question would not be included for a program that was supported by an agency or organization, which did not provide the opportunity to apply for refunding.

9. To facilitate a dialogue for the purpose of winnowing evaluation questions, Fitzpatrick et al. (2004) recommend that stakeholders be given a list of these accompanied by a short explanation regarding the importance of each.

10. Part of one criterion discussed by Fitzpatrick et al. (2004) concerns the feasibility of answering it given the availability of time.

11. The required sample sizes are somewhat higher than those indicated by Krijcie and Morgan (1970). This was done to compensate for any questionnaires that are not usable because they were completed incorrectly or have missing information. A comprehensive table of required sample sizes based on the total number in a population may be found in Krijcie and Morgan's article.

12. That stakeholders (i.e., parents) who are excluded from the sampling process may not be as supportive of a program is a real possibility. The author would like to thank Dr. Cozette Buckney, an experienced building and central office administrator, for confirming this point. Further support may be noted from *The Program Evaluation Standards* (Joint Committee on Standards, 1994), which analyzes cases, most of which are based on actual situations. One case describes a scenario where the credibility of the evaluation report was challenged, in part, because the samples were believed to be unrepresentative of their populations. It was later decided to terminate the program.

13. Along with the need for developing rapport between the interviewer and respondent, Posavac and Carey (2007) mention trust as well.

14. This step is in line with the recommendations that participation by stakeholders should be fostered in an evaluation (Fitzpatrick et al., 2004) and that they should be given the opportunity to review instruments and data collection procedures (Joint Committee on Standards, 1994).

15. Weiss (1998) also raises the point that individuals quoted in a report should not be identified without their permission.

8

The Evaluation Process:
Phases 4, 5, and 6

This chapter describes the later steps in completing an evaluation project. These involve the following phases:

- Phase 4—Analyzing data to assess a program's impact
- Phase 5—Evaluating the program's effectiveness and efficiency and offering recommendations for its future
- Phase 6—Writing the evaluation report

PHASE 4—ANALYZING DATA TO ASSESS A PROGRAM'S IMPACT

The use of quantitative and qualitative data involves different analytical approaches. These approaches complement each other, however, when conclusions are drawn from the results disclosed by responding to the evaluation questions.

The quantitative data analyses described in this section are based on the criterion of *practical significance*, rather than statistical significance. Although the latter provides more of an objective gauge for assessing a program's impact, the overriding criterion to use for weighing outcomes is one of practical significance. With this perspective, the basic question to ask for determining such significance is have the students made meaningful,[1] that is, noteworthy progress in the program being evaluated? The reason for raising this issue is that a small gain for its participants, say an average of three months, may turn out to be statistically significant if the size of the groups (e.g., innovative vs. regular) being compared is relatively large.[2]

When a difference reflects statistical significance, this means that the gap between groups would be due to chance rather than to the intervention only a very small portion of the time (e.g., five times in one hundred). However, in view of the amount of time and resources expended in implementing instructional activities, a small gain, although statistically significant, may not be considered that important. Rather than rely on evidence of program effectiveness based on a result produced by a test that is "perhaps too heavily influenced by sample size" (Urdan, 2005, p. 63), practical significance can instead be determined. Interpreting outcomes with this approach constitutes the "bottom line" in assessing the worth of a program. Therefore, "at some point, the practical significance of a result must be addressed" (Kellow, 1998, Interpreting "Significance" Via Statistical Tests section, 1). Thus the final determination of how successful a program is rests with the evaluators. Their professional judgment as educators is grounded in the collective knowledge of the team members whose experience in formally and informally assessing student achievement, attitudes, and behavior has helped prepare them for participation in an evaluation project.

It should be mentioned that relying on practical significance as the fundamental criterion for evaluating outcomes does not preclude conducting traditional statistical analyses to substantiate findings.[3] In this regard, team members knowledgeable about how to analyze computer-generated results can use a software program to determine if the mean difference in exam scores between students in different programs involving the same subject is statistically significant.

An alternative to measuring the extent to which chance accounts for a difference in achievement that does not involve the application of statistical tests is described next. As will be seen, its use provides a basis to support conclusions regarding the effectiveness and efficiency of a program being assessed.

Determining Practical Significance

A test of statistical significance (e.g., a t-test) discloses the extent to which chance is responsible for causing the difference between groups. Through this method of analyzing data, researchers hope that for the most part they can reject chance as a factor in producing the difference and instead attribute a group's higher performance to the effectiveness of one of the treatments (e.g., a particular program). In contrast, with the use of percentages, chance is not a consideration, nor are there statistical requirements that have to be met.

The quantitative analyses presented in this chapter involve the interpretation of differences in means and percentages. The former, as a measure of practical significance, is a type of *effect size* that evaluators can use to indicate the magnitude of differences between groups (Kellow, 1998).

From this perspective, percentage differences can also be placed under the umbrella of effect size in that these can disclose the extent to which one group (a) has performed relative to another and/or (b) has improved. In either situation, effect size reveals the extent to which the program being evaluated has made an impact on its participants.

Perspectives on the Use of Percentages for Analyzing Data

In order for evaluation reports to be relevant, they must be a viable source of reference to guide programmatic decisions. In this regard, conclusions drawn about the impact of a curriculum should be stated in terms that stakeholders can both easily understand and relate to.[4] Using percentages to analyze data meets these criteria because they can be readily interpreted since they have universal meaning.

Percentages provide a scale of measurement that communicates the concept of magnitude clearly across different stakeholder groups. For example, a score equivalent to 90 percent on an exam indicates excellent performance. Percentages are also easily calculated and do not require the level of understanding for their interpretation as would be the case with more technical statistical tests. Another advantage of using percentages is that they standardize the reporting of outcomes. In this way, they compensate for situations in which comparisons are made between (a) groups of unequal size and (b) tests having different content and/or numbers of possible points.

Against this background, the data analysis approaches presented next yield results that summarize the extent of (a) improvement and (b) differences between groups. As will be seen, the percentages derived from these analyses can be quickly translated into ratios, which further underscore the practical nature of these analyses.

A Short Review of Two Evaluation Approaches

Prior to discussing the use of percentages in analyzing student outcomes, it seems useful to revisit the two basic methods described in Chapter 3 for evaluating programs—nonexperimental and experimental. Recall that the former is used when it is decided to assess a program that has been in operation long enough to have made an impact. This can be determined by evidence measuring student success in either of these two situations:

- Appraising the progress of students when only one program is involved
- Comparing the difference in student outcomes when a particular curriculum is compared with another having essentially the same goals (e.g., pilot vs. regular program)

A program that has been modified, based on its assessment, would serve as the experimental group that in the future will have its outcomes compared with that of a control group composed of students in the regular program.

When applying percentages to analyze the results of nonexperimental and experimental approaches, tables serve a useful function in providing the structure for organizing and summarizing findings. Examples of various tables that correspond to the purpose of certain analytical methods are presented next.

Measuring Improvement—Two-Group Comparison

Figure 8.1 depicts the extent to which participants in one program made progress relative to their counterparts in another. The approach for analyzing the type of data shown in this figure would be appropriate for the experimental designs in Chapter 4 where comparing the gains of two groups was discussed.

Figure 8.1   A Comparison of Reading Achievement: Students Exposed to the XYZ Individualized Reading Program Versus a Basal Reader Approach

Group	N	Pretest Mean	Posttest Mean	Difference Pretest – Posttest*	Percent Improvement
XYZ	22	28.20	40.45	12.25	43
Basal	24	28.40	34.10	5.70	20

N = number of cases
*This difference is determined by subtracting the pretest from the posttest.

As evident by the categories designated in the table, a *change analysis* is involved. (Depending on the information sought, mean grade equivalent scores can instead be calculated.) The following describes how this analysis is carried out.

Examine the pretest means scores as a check on the equivalency of the groups at a particular point in time (e.g., at the beginning of the school year). These means should be nearly the same. If this is not the case, then the groups should be balanced. This can be done by deleting one or more scores from the top end of the distribution for the group with the higher mean and one or more scores from the low end for the group with the lower mean. The recalculated means of both groups should then be checked and any needed adjustments made. Note that the students who are dropped from the pretest should not be counted for the posttest analysis.

To determine the percentage of improvement for each group, subtract the mean of the pretest from that of the posttest, and divide this difference by the pretest. Thus in the case shown in Figure 8.1, each student in the innovative program improved an average of 43 percent, while for those in the basal group, the gain was only 20 percent.

Improvement Ratio

As a further measure of improvement, the ratio of percentage gain of one group over another can be calculated. This involves simply dividing the smaller percentage into the larger one. Using the values from Figure 8.1, the ratio would be $43/20 = 2.15$. Interpreted, this means that on average, students in the XYZ program improved about twice as much as their counterparts in the basal group.

Interpreting Improvement Ratios

As with any indicator of practical significance, this ratio relies on professional judgment grounded in common sense. Thus at first glance, it would seem reasonable that if one group improved twice as much as another, this would be noteworthy. However, this is not the case with a 10 percent mean gain over one of 5 percent. Therefore, one should still rely on the difference in percentage of improvement as the basis for drawing conclusions about the performance of one group versus another. A ratio derived from this difference would simply provide an additional perspective on the amount of relative gain.

As a further note, while a marked gain helps support the effectiveness of a particular program and should be recognized, it does not present the complete picture. A comprehensive program evaluation would warrant a further analysis. That is, it would also be worthwhile to see how participants in a program being evaluated measure up to a benchmark that transcends a particular school, e.g., a state standard or national norm. Without such a comparison, there is a gap in the assessment profile. Moreover, if there is a marked discrepancy between where students are relative to some standard outside of a local building, this provides a target to aim for. How a program that holds promise can be refined to meet this challenge is consistent with the benefits of what an evaluation project can yield.

Measuring Improvement—One Group

When only one program is being evaluated because there is no similar comparison group available, a pretest is necessary since it provides a base from which to measure change. This analysis is appropriate for a one-group time series experimental design as discussed in Chapter 4. The situation calls for the administration of the same pre- and posttests. Readers of the evaluation report would need to be informed of the rationale for which of the pre- and posttests were selected. In this regard, reviewing the previous material covering this design should be helpful.

Figure 8.2 illustrates a table for summarizing the results of this analysis. Using the mean difference between pre- and posttests, the ratio of percentage gain over both time periods can also be calculated.

Figure 8.2   A Comparison of Pre- and Posttest Performance of Students in an Afterschool Math Program (N = X)

	Pretest 1	Pretest 2	Posttest 1	Posttest 2	Difference Posttest 2-Pretest 2	Percent improvement
Mean	xx.xx	xx.xx	xx.xx	xx.xx	xx.xx	xx.xx

Points to Consider When Interpreting Improvement

As indicated previously, if the extent of gain is being measured, this effort can be labeled change analysis. Its use would be aligned with educators' dispositions to help students continuously improve.[5] However, the results yielded by analyzing change would be less dramatic for subjects where students are not as dependent on learning new material as in the case of reading and writing as opposed to math, science, or social studies. Thus a noticeable improvement in achievement in certain subjects may be inflated by the fact that students performed relatively low on a pretest because they were not yet taught new content.

At the time of pretesting, some students may be relatively high in achievement. Therefore, when compared to their posttest performance, they may not have demonstrated as much of a percentage gain as students whose pretest scores were lower. Thus in addition to analyzing gains, the percentages of students who were above a certain standard (e.g., grade level) on the pre- and posttests can be compared. Determining these percentages would be applicable when either one or two groups are involved in the assessment.

Other Approaches for Analyzing Data

Evaluation findings from nonexperimental or experimental methods expressed in percentage terms can be displayed in *cross-break* tables that link established categories of student performance with the programs be-ing compared.[6] Figure 8.3 illustrates how test results can be summarized in this way.

Figure 8.3   A Comparison of Science Test Performance Between Students in Modified and Regular Programs

Performance Levels and Corresponding Percentages of Items Answered Correctly	Modified Program	Regular Program
Excellent (90 +)	N = 20 26%	N = 11 14%
Good (79–89)	N = 34 44%	N = 27 34%
Fair (65–78)	N = 17 22%	N = 30 38%
Poor (below 65)	N = 6 8%	N = 12 15%
Totals	N = 77 100%	N = 80 101%*

Note: The figures within the cells represent the percentage of students in each program that achieved a particular level of test performance.

*This total exceeds 100 because of rounding that was done in certain categories.

The following describes the background for the example shown in Figure 8.3. A middle school has made substantial changes in the learning activities of a seventh-grade science curriculum and conducted an experiment to de-termine how effective the modified program was as compared to one in which students experienced the usual course of study.

Four classes were involved—two constituted the modified program (ex-perimental group) and two classes provided a basis for comparison (control group). One of the criteria of student achievement that all four teachers agreed to for evaluating the modified program was a department test consisting of the material from five units. The total number of points earned by each stu-dent over the entire set of exams served as the outcome variable. (Recall from Chapter 4 that such scores would also be known as the dependent variable. The two programs would make up the independent variable.)

By consensus, all teachers established the standards indicated in Figure 8.3 as constituting the various levels of test performance. How to summarize what students in the program being evaluated were able to achieve relative to their peers in the comparison group is discussed next.

Reporting the Results of a Cross-Break Table

To interpret outcomes displayed in a cross-break table, examine the percentages in the cells across programs to determine if a trend in the data might be present. This can be identified by combining the results of two categories to indicate where the larger percentage of cases occurred for the evaluated program. A frame of reference would then be established for comparing students in this group with those in the regular program. Thus by examining Figure 8.3, it can be concluded that 70 percent of students (N = 54) in the modified program obtained good or excellent exam scores as compared to 48 percent of those (N = 38) in the regular program. The extent of difference in the lowest category should also be indicated. For example, this could be stated as follows: A larger percentage of students who failed the test were from the regular program (15 percent, N = 12) as compared to their counterparts in the modified program (8 percent, N = 6).

While combining performance categories is used for summarizing results, a particular finding can also be highlighted if a noticeable difference is present in a single category. Different levels of student mastery could also be profiled by classifying results as illustrated in the example shown in Figure 8.4.

Figure 8.4 A Profile of Reading Achievement: XYZ Individualized Reading Program Versus a Basal Reader Method

Group	N	Mastered less than 75% of material	Mastered 76-85% of material	Mastered over 85% of material	Total %*
Whole language	49	N = 6 % = 12	N = 32 % = 65	N = 11 % = 22	99%
Phonics	52	N = 2 % = 4	N = 31 % = 60	N = 19 % = 37	101%

*All percentages are rounded to the nearest whole number.

Regarding the analyses shown in Figures 8.3 and 8.4: They would not be used to measure gain since no pretest was given. However, a check should be made to determine if the groups were comparable in ability at a previous time (e.g., at the beginning of the school year). Means based on original (raw) scores or grade equivalent scores can be used for this purpose.

Connecting Numbers and Percentages

It is important to indicate the number of individuals that correspond to each percentage reported. Doing so gives a more complete "picture" of the results. As an example, for a program that has sixty students, it was found that 20 percent of its participants obtained excellent grades. However, without the number of students known, to what does this percent translate? Thus also reporting how many individuals represent the percentage provides more meaning to the interpretation of the results.

Determining the Effect of a Program on Specific Groups

Another way cross-break tables can be used is for comparing results of students representing different ability levels in one program with their counterparts in another. This analysis discloses if a particular program has produced a differential effect on one or more subgroups (Joint Committee on Standards, 1994). Thus by disaggregating data, it can be determined if participants having a certain characteristic perform particularly well (Weiss, 1998). In this regard, the following discusses how a cross-break analysis can be applied to enable this determination.

Assume that 78 percent of the students in a math pilot program met or exceeded state standards versus 59 percent of those in a regular program. A difference of 19 percentage points reflects a noticeable gap between the groups. However, what would these figures reveal if the data were disaggregated according to ability level of the students as determined by classifying them independently of their performance on the state test? For example, students in each program could be assigned to subgroups on the basis of their most recent standardized test scores. As shown in Figure 8.5, the criterion used for dividing students into two categories was whether each was below or at or above grade level according to the national norm for the subject. (Another approach for establishing different ability levels is shown in Figure 8.6.)

Figure 8.5   Percentages of Students at Different Ability Levels in Programs That Have Met or Exceeded State Math Standards

	PILOT PROGRAM N = 58		REGULAR PROGRAM N = 57	
	At or above grade level N = 30	Below grade level N = 28	At or above grade level N = 29	Below grade level N = 28
Meets or exceeds State standards	N = 26 87%	N = 19 68%	N = 22 76%	N = 11 39%
Does not meet State standards	N = 4 13%	N = 9 32%	N = 7 24%	N = 17 61%
Total percent	100 %	100%	100%	100%

It can be concluded that the pilot program made a greater impact on be-low grade level students. This was determined by comparing the percent-ages found in the cells for the subgroups across both programs. The difference for lower ability students was noticeably larger (24 percent) than that found when the high-ability subgroups were compared (13 percent).

Along the lines indicated by the Joint Committee on Standards (1994), differentiating data serves to eliminate the masking of differences when only overall results are examined. Thus a more focused analysis provides a basis for determining direction for the subsequent delivery of a program. As applied to the situation being illustrated, the results support the worth of the program, especially for the lower ability students. However, the per-centages of the more able participants in the pilot program relative to their peers in the regular curriculum would suggest that ways to modify learn-ing activities and materials be implemented which are designed to raise achievement of new (or continuing) upper-level students. Such efforts can enhance a program's potential. From an outcomes perspective, gearing teaching and learning approaches according to need is fundamental to el-evating performance.

Before leaving this discussion, it should be pointed out that a prescrip-tive/diagnostic approach is called for regarding those students who have demonstrated substandard performance. This would apply to participants in both programs. However, regarding the pilot program (or any that is be-ing assessed), the evaluation team should suggest as a recommendation for improving the program that possible factors be identified as to why a num-ber of students have not made satisfactory progress. Proactive strategies should then be incorporated in delivering the program to prevent or lessen the likelihood of this situation reoccurring. The need for such identification is highlighted, especially when higher ability students are not successful.

Figure 8.6 Determining the Effectiveness of the Experimental Treatment by Comparing Subgroups

Steps:

1. Combine the scores of students in the experimental and regular programs based on a recent exam both groups have taken (e.g., the latest standardized test). Next, calculate the overall mean.

2. Using this mean, form two groups by categorizing students according to whether or not their score was at or above average (higher ability) or below average (lower ability).

3. Separate higher ability students in the combined group according to their participation in either the experimental or the regular program. Do the same for the lower ability students. There are now four subgroups as shown in the following crossbreak table:

	Program	
Student Level	Experimental	Regular
Higher ability		
Lower ability		

Note that classifying students to form subgroups can also be extended to other variables besides achievement, e.g., attitudes toward a subject as measured by a questionnaire.

Other Outcome Variables

An approach for a one- or two-group analysis is to compare report card data for two marking periods. These constitute the pre-and post-observation periods. For example, the percentage of students earning *A*s and *B*s could be compared. Including the first marking period serves as a base from which the extent of improvement or consistency in student achievement can be determined. Therefore, the students should be the same for the pre-measures and post-measures. If participants have joined the group after the "pre-" period, they should not be included in the analysis. Use the format shown in Figure 8.7 to summarize these analyses. If only one group is involved in the evaluation, the table format can still be used but without the second row.

Figure 8.7 A Comparison of Report Card Grades Over Two Marking Periods Between the Interdisciplinary and Regular Social Studies Programs

Group	Total number in Program	Percent earning As and Bs		Difference in %
		1st marking period	4th marking period	
Interdisciplinary				
Regular				

When overall exam results are also available by subtests (e.g., math computation and word problems) these scores should be reported as well. Doing so adds to the comprehensiveness of evaluation evidence. Such information would disclose if and where the program being assessed was particularly effective. For this analysis, a cross-break table can be used to examine, for example, the mean grade equivalent scores of experimental and control groups.

Another illustration involves using a nonstandardized test that provides disaggregated data. Based on an agreed upon standard that constitutes satisfactory performance, the percentages of students across both groups can be compared.

Analyzing Observational Data

The steps shown in Figure 8.8 can be used to analyze and interpret observational data. The procedure is based on the fourteen-item instrument introduced in Chapter 7 (Figure 7.4) that uses a five-option continuum to assess student performance. These steps apply to a situation in which classes in an innovative program are being observed. However, the process is repeated if a comparison group is involved.

Prior to making any observations, it would be useful for the raters to review each item on the observation scale and discuss the type of student responses that would constitute the different ratings on the five-option continuum. After the first session, the observers should compare ratings to determine the extent to which they are discrepant. If there are marked differences between them, these should be discussed with a view toward understanding why each made their particular judgment. Comments made in the space provided under each item should be useful for this purpose. Better understanding may reduce differences that could occur on the second observation. If noticeable differences are consistent, this finding should be indicated in the evaluation report since it would lessen the reliability of the observations.

Figure 8.8 Procedure for Analyzing Observational Data

Step:

1. Total the ratings of all items on the instrument assigned by each rater for the first observation and add these values.

2. Divide by 2 to obtain an average for Observation 1.

3. Divide this average by the number of items on the instrument to obtain the mean for the first observation from both raters. The result yields the average overall rating for each item in terms of the five point scale.

4. Repeat steps 1, 2, and 3 for Observation 2. (Repeat again should a third observation be made.)

5. Find the overall mean rating given by both observers for each item by dividing the results from steps 3 and 4 by the number of observations made.

An illustration of this procedure is shown next. In this situation, assume that there is only one staff member teaching in a pilot program.* If two or more teachers are involved, an average rating would be obtained to represent their classes.

	Observation 1	Observation 2
Total rating from Rater A	56	59
Total rating from Rater B	+ 60	+ 62
Total of ratings from the observation	116	121
Average rating from the observation (÷2)	58	60.5
Average overall rating for each item (÷14)	4.14	4.32

To obtain the overall mean of the items from both observations:

$$\frac{\text{Average item rating from Observation 1}}{2} + \frac{\text{Average item rating from Observation 2}}{2} \quad \text{or} \quad \frac{4.14}{2} + \frac{4.32}{2} = \frac{8.46}{2} = 4.23$$

On a 5-point scale, this result can be interpreted as a high rating. For situations in which more than one teacher was observed, the result obtained in step 5 for each teacher would be combined and averaged. For example:

Overall mean rating for each item—Teacher 1	4.10
Overall mean rating for each item—Teacher 2	+ 4.20
	8.30
	÷ 2
Overall mean ratings for each item—Teachers 1 and 2	4.15

*The same procedure would be followed if a comparison group was involved.

Results of observations can be used for formative and summative purposes. Regarding the latter, the overall score obtained on the rating scale can serve as an indicator of program effectiveness. Formatively, item-by-item analyses could suggest areas for faculty efforts to improve student performance concerning interactions with their teachers and other students. These analyses can contribute information concerning the team's recommendations for improving program processes—the diagnostic function of evaluation. An item analysis could also support a favorable assessment by the team as to the program's particular strengths—the confirming function of evaluation. Figure 8.9 illustrates this type of analysis. Also note that if an experiment is implemented for a modified program, pre- and post-observations can be conducted to determine the extent of improvement following the approach used when achievement data are analyzed to measure change.

Figure 8.9 Item Analysis for Observational Data

Item I	Rater A	Rater B
Observation 1	3	2
Observation 2	+ 4	+ 3
Total	7	5
Average for item from the Rater (Total ÷ 2 observations)	3.5	2.5
Average overall rating for item (Rater A average + Rater B average ÷ 2)	3.5 + 2.5 = 6 ÷ 2 = 3	

Attention is now drawn to Figure 8.10, which shows how average ratings assigned by observers can be displayed on an item-by-item basis and over the entire instrument.

Figure 8.10 Observer Ratings of Classroom Interactions Between Two Programs

Item	Mean Rating	
Students	Modified Program	Regular Program
1. were actively engaged in the learning process	x.xx	x.xx
2. responded well to the teacher's questions	x.xx	x.xx
3. raised *how* and *why* questions	x.xx	x.xx
4. were attentive when the teacher gave explanations	x.xx	x.xx
5. appeared well prepared for the lesson	x.xx	x.xx
6. displayed appropriate classroom behavior	x.xx	x.xx
7. appeared to be interested in the lesson	x.xx	x.xx
8. used their time productively	x.xx	x.xx
9. responding to the teacher's questions was not limited to a few individuals	x.xx	x.xx
10. demonstrated understanding of the lesson by their responses	x.xx	x.xx
11. held an effective dialogue with the teacher	x.xx	x.xx
12. held an effective dialogue with each other	x.xx	x.xx
13. made appropriate references to the text	x.xx	x.xx
14. were able to use learning material besides the text effectively	x.xx	x.xx
Overall mean rating	x.xx	x.xx

Analyzing Attitudinal Data

As was the case with observational data, the responses to an instrument measuring attitudes toward a subject can be used summatively and formatively. For the latter, an item-by-item analysis can disclose the percentages of students that chose various options on a Likert scale as shown in the following example for fifty students:

The work I do in science is interesting.

	Strongly agree	Agree	Not sure	Disagree	Strongly disagree
N =	3	7	8	22	10
% =	6	14	16	44	20

Disaggregating the data in this way could contribute information for improving the program's operation.

An overall group mean can also be obtained to provide summative evidence of student attitudes as outlined in Figure 8.11. When interpreting an overall mean on an attitude questionnaire with a five-point Likert scale format, a judgment should be made in verbal terms that translates what the average response represents. For example, a mean of 4.2 can be categorized as "good" attitudes, but 3.2 as "neutral."

Figure 8.11 Calculating an Overall Mean for Attitude Questionnaires

---

Assume that a ten-item questionnaire with a five-option Likert scale was given to fifty students.

Steps

1. Score each questionnaire according to how the scale was weighted. In this example, since five choices were possible, the most positive response would be worth five points. (See pg. 108 for examples of how positively and negatively worded items would be scored.)

2. Add the scores obtained for all of the questionnaires completed by the group. Let's assume that the scores for the fifty questionnaires produced a total of 2,100 points.

3. Divide the total points by the number of questionnaires. For this example: 2100 ÷ 50 = 42. This yields the *average total score* (ATS) for each participant.

4. Divide the ATS by the number of items on the questionnaire. This will translate the ATS into a value that can be located on the original scale used to record responses. In this case, 42 ÷ 10 = 4.2 which reflects the *average response* assigned by each participant to the entire questionnaire.

Note: In illustrating these steps, only one group was involved. For a two-group comparison, the same process would enable one to examine the extent to which the groups differed overall.

Student opinions about a certain subject reflect attitudes toward it in general. Using a Likert scale, statements referring to the curriculum being evaluated could be added to a student survey and an item analysis applied. The following is an example where the frame of reference is a particular program:

The honors program in English has helped me improve my writing.

Certain items can also be taken from the questionnaire if they address a particular evaluation question. Their individual means would then be reported.

Analyzing Opinions of Parents

The process described in Figure 8.11 can also be applied to analyzing responses from parents on a questionnaire used in determining program effectiveness. As with a student survey, items can also be analyzed individually if they are appropriate for a particular evaluation question. Furthermore, a two-group comparison can be made between parents of students participating in the program being evaluated and parents of those in the regular program.

Using Graphs to Display Results

In addition to tables summarizing student outcomes, graphs can be incorporated into an evaluation report to supplement the presentation of findings. Their advantage is that they show a more vivid picture overall of group differences. However, because they are constructed with calibrations in standard units, graphs are not able to illustrate findings exactly the way tables can. This point notwithstanding, graphs could further reinforce the evidence depicted in a table. Thus after conclusions are drawn based on information presented in a table, an accompanying graph can display results to produce a stronger impression. At the same time, not every table requires a corresponding graph. In this regard, the use of graphs should be considered when it is felt that an additional illustration would help dramatize the extent of differences found. As a further point, tables are also not always needed if results being reported are very brief.

A "picture" of the results can easily be constructed using word processing software by accessing the help menu and following the directions for creating "charts." Presented is a chart that can serve as a template in which the categories shown can be substituted with the designations used in a table. Figures 8.12 and 8.13 contain examples of a type of diagram—a bar graph—that can accompany a table.

Figure 8.12 A Comparison of Reading Test Scores Between Two Programs: XYZ Individualized Reading and Basal Reader

Group	N	Pretest Mean	Posttest Mean	Difference Pretest-Posttest *	Percent Improvement
XYZ	22	28.20	40.45	12.25	.43
Basal	24	28.40	34.10	5.70	.20

N = number of cases

*Note: This difference is determined by subtracting the pretest from the posttest.

A Graphic Representation of Figure 8.12

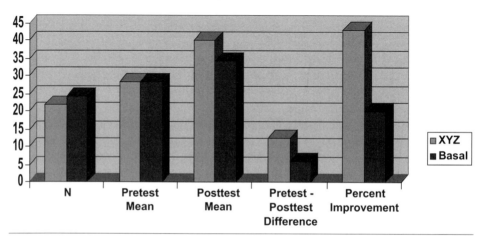

Figure 8.13 illustrates how findings can be presented when a criterion-referenced test has been given. The percentages defining the categories reflect different levels of content mastery. Note that what constitutes a minimum standard for acceptable performance (in this case 75 percent mastery) should be determined by the team in consultation with the staff of both programs. Other cut-off points would also be ascertained by consensus.

Figure 8.13 A Profile of Reading Test Performance Between Whole
Language and Phonics Programs

Group	N	Mastered less than 75% of material	Mastered 76–85% of material	Mastered over 85% of material	Total %*
Whole language	49	N = 6 % = 12	N = 32 % = 65	N = 11 % = 22	99%
Phonics	52	N = 2 % = 4	N = 31 % = 60	N = 19 % = 37	101%

*All percentages are rounded to the nearest whole number.

A Graphic Representation of Figure 8.13

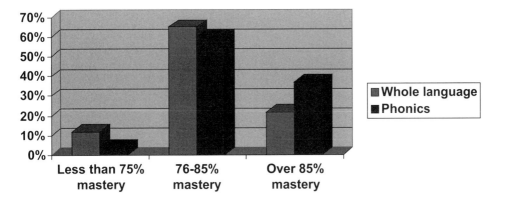

Analyzing Qualitative Data

Qualitative information provides the in-depth dimension of the evaluation study. In analyzing open-ended questions from survey questionnaires or those posed during interviews, search for patterns in the data to determine if there is a majority position. For example, state that eight of the ten parents interviewed felt that the program helped their children develop more interest in reading at home. Next, provide a few representative direct quotes that support the respondents' opinions, even those that may be dissenting.

In conducting interviews, analyzing responses would be facilitated if a scale were to accompany certain questions. For example, suppose that an interviewee was asked the following:

How effective was the pilot program in helping students understand the material?

These options could then be presented to elicit a response:

Very effective, effective, somewhat effective, and not very effective

A count of the responses will disclose if a clear pattern of opinions exist. While opinions can be readily summarized with this technique, the respondents should also be asked to explain their answers. Such additional information, as previously stated, can provide insights into an individual's perspectives and is therefore consistent with the rationale for obtaining qualitative data. In this regard, representative comments should be included in the report.

For focus group interviews, since the opinions of individuals are not being tallied with respect to a particular survey question (e.g., how many answered positively), it will be necessary for the interviewers to ascertain the overall reaction to the group's responses. This can be done by reiterating what the interviewer believes the respondents' position is on a question raised. Thus a statement such as the following can summarize reactions: "From your comments, it seems that all (or most) of you agree that the pilot program you used in teaching science was very effective. Does anyone disagree?" Again, a few representative comments would support the group's position. If there were any dissenting opinions, this should be noted, and comments typical of those disagreeing should also be included. As stated previously, where applicable, an evaluation question should be answered by obtaining both quantitative and qualitative information. The results of analyses involving both of these sources of data enable a more comprehensive evaluation than if only one approach was used.

PHASE 5—EVALUATING THE PROGRAM'S EFFECTIVENESS AND OFFERING RECOMMENDATIONS FOR ITS FUTURE

In this phase, the team examines all of the qualitative and quantitative evidence and then, through consensus, makes an assessment concerning the program's overall effectiveness (e.g., "very effective" or "somewhat effective"). Drawing such a conclusion calls for professional judgment by the team members. For example, if students in a remedial program make an eight-month gain on a standardized test over those who did not have this experience, how should such improvement be designated? Would the team regard this growth as "marked" or "excellent"? Whatever the label assigned to student development, it should characterize the extent to which the program is meeting its goals.

The exception to waiting for evaluation criteria to emerge is the case when an objective has been formulated at the beginning of the program, as shown in the following example:

> At least 75 percent of the students participating in the afterschool reading program will increase their grade equivalent scores by a minimum of six months.

The extent to which an objective such as the preceding has been achieved can be readily measured. As such, it provides more objective evidence to support the team's evaluation. Other aspects to weigh in making this judgment are discussed next.

Considering the Program's Context

A variety of factors found in the setting (i.e., context) in which the program is operating can affect its outcomes in addition to the instructional processes that are part of the curriculum. According to the Joint Committee on Standards (1994), contextual factors should be acknowledged when interpreting the findings of an evaluation since they can influence the extent to which a program is successful.

A number of these factors were included in the program needs assessment presented in Chapter 7. Where responses from items reflect a consensus for "medium" and "high" priority for change, this information can provide a basis for qualifying the overall evaluation by the team of the program's effectiveness. Thus when judgment is less than excellent, it would be tempered by the constraints on the program's operation (e.g., students lacking basic skills in the subject) identified in the needs assessment.

If an evaluation is qualified in some way, this should be indicated in the report along with a statement of the possible potential of the curriculum for producing better student outcomes when certain program needs are met. Including this position held by the team should enhance the credibility of the report because it is likely to be perceived as a fair appraisal. As a further note, the source for qualifying any judgment should not be limited to the information obtained by the program needs assessment. As discussed earlier, an evaluation question to elicit recommendations for improving the program from the staff may also identify factors concerning the context in which the curriculum is being delivered.

Considering the Program's Efficiency

Another issue in evaluating a program is the school's resources—time and financial—that were expended in preparing for and implementing instructional activities. This is the efficiency dimension of the evaluation for which the issue of program worth is addressed based on opinions elicited by the following evaluation question (which was raised in Chapter 7):

- Are the outcomes produced by the program worth the time and/or money expended to prepare for and implement it?

By determining a trend in responses to this question, the team can draw a conclusion about perceptions of the program's worth held by program staff and the administrator(s). To facilitate identifying this trend, a scale with options such as the following can accompany this question: well worth it, worth it, and not worth it. Respondents should also be asked to explain their choice. This additional perspective might disclose a specific reason to support why they felt a certain way. For example,

- "the program did not require a great deal of preparation time";
- "the program costs were reasonable considering the benefits that students received"; and
- "less class time was spent explaining learning activities as compared to other programs."

By ascertaining where most individuals stand on the issue of a program's worth, relative to what it took to deliver it, the team is then in a better position to recommend whether efforts should be directed at finding a program that might be more efficient, that is, one that would not require as many resources to implement. The resource issue is treated in the conclusion section of the evaluation report. Conclusions drawn about a program's effectiveness and efficiency, including recommendations for its improvement, are part of this report and are covered further in Chapter 9.

Responding to Evaluation Questions

Among other functions, these questions guide decisions for determining the types of data to be collected and analyzed. As can be seen in Figure 8.14, the data obtained should represent various sources of information that would help ensure that the team possesses reasonable evidence to support its judgment and recommendations. In this regard, the extent to which qualitative results are consistent with those obtained from quantitative analyses serve to corroborate the team's position.

Figure 8.14 is organized according to the questions that can be raised in an assessment study—outcome and generic. The former are aligned with a program's goals (including objectives if stated). Generic issues raised are applicable to different curriculums. Both forms of questions enable appraising a program's worth and operation and therefore, are congruent with the approach for evaluating programs presented in this book.

PHASE 6—WRITING THE EVALUATION REPORT

Present the document to stakeholders in two stages: draft and final forms. Consistent with Fitzpatrick et al. (2004). For the draft version, elicit feedback from stakeholders concerning the quality of the report and any of its aspects that might need to be clarified. Ask respondents for their critical comments about the soundness and usefulness of the report. Consider this feedback carefully for the final version.

As a further note, providing the opportunity for stakeholders to lend input for the final version promotes ownership of the evaluation project. Thus involving them increases the likelihood of gaining support for the team's conclusions and recommendations.[7]

Figure 8.14 A Synthesis of Data Collection and Analysis Procedures*

Evaluation Question	Source of Information	Type of Data Collected	Method of Data Collection	Method of Analyzing Data**
Outcome (Each question reflecting its corresponding program goal is listed.)	Students Program staff Program Coordinator (if applicable) Administrator(s) Parents	Quantitative Qualitative	Obtain test scores and grades for student assignments from the program staff. Distribute questionnaires. Conduct individual and/or focus group interviews with students, program staff, and administrator(s).	Calculate means and percentages. Interpret extent of differences. Calculate ratios where applicable. Identify if a trend in opinions exist by counting responses recorded on a scale for questions posed during interviews and for questionnaire items. Summarize reactions to question raised. Determine if there is consensus on positions expressed on issues.
Were there positive outcomes that occurred that were not indicated in the goal statements?	Program staff Program Coordinator	Qualitative	Conduct individual or focus group interviews.	Summarize the most typical response by indicating what individuals are generally stating. Determine if there is consensus on opinions.
Are there features of the program that were especially useful in helping students learn?	Program staff Program Coordinator	Qualitative	Conduct individual or focus group interviews.	Same as above.

(Continued)

Figure 8.14 (continued)

Evaluation Question	Source of Information	Type of Data Collected	Method of Data Collection	Method of Analyzing Data**
Are the outcomes produced by the program worth the time and/or money expended to prepare for and implement it?	Program staff Program Coordinator Administrator(s)	Quantitative Qualitative	Conduct individual or focus group interviews.	Summarize the most typical response by indicating what individuals are generally stating. Identify if a trend in opinions exists by counting responses recorded on a scale used for this question.
Are there recommendations for improving the program?	Program staff Program Coordinator	Qualitative	Conduct individual or focus group interviews.	Summarize the most typical response, but also report other recommendations.
Should the program continue in its present form, be modified, or be replaced with one that appears more promising?	Program staff Program Coordinator Administrator(s)	Quantitative Qualitative	Conduct individual or focus group interviews.	Count responses according to the three options presented. Summarize the most typical response by indicating what individuals are generally stating.

* All but one of the categories shown in this figure are contained in some form among those included in a work sheet presented by Fitzpatrick et al. (2004) for summarizing an evaluation plan.

** Not all of the methods indicated need to be employed for each group from which data are collected.

One important step is to include an acknowledgment page thanking stakeholders for their input and cooperation in copies of the report that are disseminated to them. As stated earlier, confidentiality and anonymity should be maintained.

Make necessary revisions for the final report. Proofread the document and submit it to appropriate audiences. Chapter 9 contains a format for an evaluation report that connects all six phases of the evaluation process.

CHAPTER 8 HIGHLIGHTS

1.   Quantitative and qualitative data analyses complement each other when conclusions are drawn from the results disclosed by responding to the evaluation questions.

2.   To determine practical significance, calculating percentage differences as a measure of effect size can disclose the extent to which one group has (a) performed relative to another and/or (b) improved.

3.   As an additional measure of improvement, the ratio of percentage gain of one group over another can be calculated.

4.   Evaluation findings expressed in percentage terms can be displayed in cross-break tables that link established categories of student performance with the programs being compared.

5.   Another way cross-break tables can be used is for comparing results of students representing different ability levels in one program with their counterparts in another.

6.   Results of observations and those obtained from attitude questionnaires can be used summatively and formatively.

7.   In addition to tables summarizing student outcomes, graphs can be incorporated into an evaluation report to supplement the presentation of findings.

8.   Qualitative information provides the in-depth dimension of an evaluation study by obtaining explanations from respondents as to the effectiveness of the program being evaluated.

9.   Through consensus, the evaluation team judges the overall effectiveness of the program and also provides its own and others' recommendations for improvement. Considering the context in which the program operates and its efficiency are also aspects the team would consider in judging its worth.

10. The evaluation report should be presented to stakeholders in two stages: draft and final forms. During the first stage, critical comments should be elicited from stakeholders and their feedback carefully considered for the final version.

NOTES

1. Hanes and Hail (1999) use meaningful value to the client as one of the indicators for evaluating program outcomes. Along these lines, Fitzpatrick et al. (2004) indicate that a standard for evaluating programs should reflect a difference in performance that "would be considered is sufficiently meaningful" (p. 251) to stakeholders.

2. When a statistical test is applied, the size of the group(s) can affect the result. This situation is treated in many evaluation and statistics works (e.g., Fitzpatrick et al., 2004; Kellow, 1998; Urdan, 2005; Vaughn, 1998).

3. While Kellow (1998) provides a rationale for the importance of using effect size measures, in citing Maxwell, Camp, and Avery, he indicates that such measures should augment traditional tests of significance.

4. That stakeholders should be able to understand the interpretation of evaluation results is indicated by Posavac and Carey (2007). In this regard, these authors recommend that, along with statistical analyses, percentages or, even better, graphs be used to illustrate findings. The position taken in this book is that percentages should be the primary tool to analyze quantitative data for the reasons given in this chapter. At the same time, of course, graphs can also incorporate percentages. The former can also be effective to illustrate the extent of differences because of the visual impact they can make.

5. In the context of discussing methods for estimating practical significance, Kellow (1998) indicates that gains by program participants would be intuitively appealing.

6. Among the approaches used for summarizing quantitative data discussed by Gredler (1996), she includes percentages and cross-break tables.

7. In referring to interim reports given to stakeholders, Fitzpatrick et al. (2004) point out the value of sharing results and seeking their reactions. In this regard, these authors maintain that meetings with stakeholders to discuss interim findings increase the credibility of the evaluator, the evaluation, and its influence.

9

Writing the Evaluation Report

How relevant, credible, and ultimately usable the evaluation is to stakeholders depends in large measure on the quality of the evaluation report.[1] In this regard, based on the works of Fitzpatrick et al. (2004) and Owens (1979), this chapter provides a framework for organizing the report to facilitate the writing of a professional document. Note that the descriptions of what should be contained in the various sections of the report are stated as general guidelines. The writers can, of course, modify the language to suit their own preference and style.

The parts of the report to address are shown in Figure 9.1.

FORMAT AND CONTENT

I. Title Page
An example of a title page is shown in Figure 9.2.

II. Acknowledgments
The evaluation team thanks various individuals and groups for their input, cooperation, and/or support of the project.

Figure 9.1   Contents of the Evaluation Report

   I.   Title Page

   II. Acknowledgments

   III. Abstract

   IV. Purposes of the Evaluation

   V. Program Description

   VI. Evaluation Questions

   VII. Procedures for Collecting and Analyzing Evaluation Data

   VIII.Evaluation Results and Interpretation

   IX. Conclusions and Recommendations

   X. Appendices

Figure 9.2   Model of Title Page

An Evaluation of the _____ Program

at the

_____ School

A Report Submitted by the (year) Evaluation Team

    Team Leader: _____

    Members: _____

                          _____

                          _____

                          _____

Month, Year

III. Abstract

The abstract represents a summary (about two pages) of the entire evaluation report written in the past tense. It is not divided into sections with titles. The following should be included:

    A. Indicate that a systematic and comprehensive evaluation was conducted to determine the extent to which the goals of the program were (are being) achieved. (The major goals are stated here.) In the same paragraph, provide a brief description of the program. Also give the time frame during which the study was conducted (e.g., from October through April of the current school year).

    B. State that evaluation questions were raised and addressed to guide the project and obtain different types of evidence to determine the program's effectiveness.

    C. In three separate paragraphs, summarize sections VII through IX. Tables are not presented.

IV. Purposes of the Evaluation

The purposes were: to determine the effectiveness of the program and to provide recommendations for its future.[2]

V. Program Description

Include the description developed in Phase 1—Describing the Program. Specify how it was obtained, that is, by interviewing program staff and examining program materials.

VI. Evaluation Questions

Point out that responses to these questions provided a basis for drawing conclusions and making recommendations concerning various aspects of the program's impact and delivery. Also describe the procedures for formulating and selecting evaluation questions related to the program's goals. In addition, indicate that a set of generic questions were also raised to obtain further information about the program's worth and operation. Provide a list of both types of questions.

VII. Procedures for Collecting and Analyzing Evaluation Information

Methods of collecting data. Indicate the time period, that is, the month and year, during which data collection occurred. State the number of participants that were involved for each type of data collected. (Include the way sampling was done, if applicable.) Also specify how the data were collected by summarizing the techniques used, for example, interviews, survey questionnaires, and observations. In addition,

    A. provide the sources for test scores (indicate name and/or type of test, a short description of the abilities measured, number of points possible, and when taken),

    B. provide the sources for any other type of data obtained from student records, and

C. refer the reader to an appendix to examine a specimen of a survey instrument.

Data analysis methods. Separately describe quantitative and qualitative approaches used to summarize and interpret information. For the quantitative analyses, include the following:

- Where a questionnaire was used to survey opinions or attitudes, explain how the instrument was scored
- How measures (i.e., means and/or percentages) were applied to summarize opinions or attitudes and student performance

For qualitative data, explain how trends in responses were determined.

Report the percentage of usable questionnaires that were returned (or collected) based on the number of forms distributed. This percentage provides an indication of how representative the responses are with respect to the population surveyed. If the return rate is relatively low, then any conclusions drawn about opinions should be reported as tentative.

VIII. Evaluation Results and Interpretation

A. The section is introduced by informing the reader that the results will be organized according to each evaluation question.[3] Then, state each question followed by a transitional sentence such as "Information regarding this question is indicated in the following table." Also include the results of any qualitative analyses that were used under the appropriate question.

B. If they occurred, include a discussion of any other positive outcomes or negative aspects of the program. This is the last paragraph in the section.

IX. Conclusions and Recommendations

A. Evaluate the overall effectiveness of the program. For example, state that the program is (was) very effective in achieving its goals. When making any judgment, also describe the criteria that were applied.

B. Discuss the strengths of the program. Identify which aspects of it should continue as they are currently being implemented. Also provide recommendations for improvement. These should include suggestions obtained from the program staff as well as those offered by the evaluation team. Any that were given by the former should be credited to them. Recommendations should be introduced by a phrase such as

Three teachers recommended that . . .

The evaluation team recommends the following . . . (A list then follows.)

Each suggestion offered by the team should be briefly supported by giving the corresponding reason for making it. If the program has been completed, indicate what steps should be taken to improve it (or a similar one) if it were to start up in the future.

In the case where teachers delivering the program feel that it should be replaced, the report obviously would not contain recommendations for its improvement. However, the team still needs to determine the extent to which other evidence supports the staff's position. This effort enhances the objectivity of the report and thereby, makes it more creditable. A sound evaluation report that can corroborate the opinions of the staff has the value-added benefit of helping to justify (a) taking additional time to select a more promising curriculum and (b) the cost incurred for its adoption, including any funds for additional inservice if needed to help ensure that it is implemented well.

The task of searching for a better program can be made easier by incorporating representative comments in the report that accompany a question posed to the staff during interviews held with an evaluation team member. An issue raised was whether the program should be replaced (part of evaluation question 8 discussed in Chapters 7 and 8). These comments can disclose or suggest features of a program to look for that would be present in the selection of a better alternative.

C. If the assessment of the program was qualified in some way because it was operating in less than favorable conditions (e.g., being handicapped by students with deficiencies in basic skills) then, as indicated in Chapter 7, discuss the context in which the curriculum was delivered. This would support a recommendation to direct attention to the factor(s) external to the program itself that prevent it from functioning more effectively.

D. Report the overall position of the staff members concerning the program's efficiency. Recall from Chapters 7 and 8 that this involves eliciting their perspectives on the issue of whether the outcomes produced by the program was worth the time and/or money expended to prepare for and implement it.

X. Appendices

Include specimen copies of instruments (e.g., survey questionnaire, interview questionnaire, attitude measure, and an observation scale). For each instrument used, include a separate appendix with an appropriate title sheet.

WHAT THE EVALUATION REPORT REPRESENTS

The report is the culminating product of an evaluation study. As such, it should not only be clearly written (Fitzpatrick et al., 2004; Joint Committee on Standards, 1994; Weiss, 1998), but it should also provide a basis to support the conclusions and recommendations. This will contribute to the report's acceptance and usefulness. To achieve these ends, when it is recommended that a curriculum be continued, the report should highlight the two basic functions of program evaluation stated in Chapter 1: confirming the extent to which a program is effective and diagnosing areas in which improvements are needed. The reasons why these functions are pivotal are discussed next.

- **Confirming.** When a program evaluation identifies outcomes indicating how those implementing the curriculum have been successful, this serves as recognition from peers—an important source of gratification for professionals.
- **Diagnosing.** Based on objectively analyzed evidence,[4] modifications that appear promising are offered to improve areas of the curriculum and thereby provide direction for its future delivery. Such suggestions are likely to be perceived as useful since they could facilitate the teaching/learning process. Moreover, the report should be more readily accepted because it would also contain recommendations given by those implementing the program. Seeking their input is in keeping with the need for stakeholders to feel ownership in the evaluation study as advocated by Fitzpatrick et al. (2004).

In essence, the report should be respected for its excellence, fairness,[5] and professionalism by those who are responsible for implementing the curriculum within a school, by administrators in the district, and by other stakeholder groups—parents and community members—whose interest in and support of school efforts are vital.

As indicated earlier, program evaluation conducted by practitioners in a local school involves reflective practice. This applies to the evaluators, as well as those who carry out and administer the program as each group engages in thought and dialogue about instructional activities and implications of student outcomes. As a result of this process, the evaluation report should represent a viable reference from which administrators and faculty (including future evaluation team members) can learn. Its use in this regard is compatible with the disposition for continual growth characteristic of those who function in a learning organization.

In this context, writing the report can also serve as a professional development activity for the evaluation team as it proceeds in addressing the contents of the document. To guide this effort, the checklist shown in Figure 9.3 can be used for completing the report.[6]

Figure 9.3   Evaluation Report Checklist

PART I: REPORT CONTENTS

I. Title Page

❏ Does the title page contain the type of information shown in the model (Figure 9.2)?

II. Acknowledgments

❏ Have all individuals and groups involved been mentioned?

III. Abstract

A. Have the following been indicated?
   ❏ That a systematic and comprehensive evaluation was conducted
   ❏ The extent to which goals were (or are being) achieved
   ❏ The major goals
   ❏ A brief description of the program
   ❏ The time frame for the study

B. Were evaluation questions raised for the following?
   ❏ To guide the project
   ❏ To obtain different types of evidence to determine program effectiveness

C. Three separate paragraphs should summarize the following (which correspond to sections VII, VIII, and IX of the report, respectively).
   ❏ Procedures for collecting and analyzing evaluation information
   ❏ Evaluation results and interpretation
   ❏ Conclusions

IV. Purposes of the Evaluation

Have the following purposes of the evaluation been stated?
   ❏ To determine the effectiveness of the program
   ❏ To provide recommendations for its future

V. Program Description

❏ Has the program description been included?
❏ Was information given on how the description was obtained?

VI. Evaluation Questions

❏ Were the procedures for formulating and selecting evaluation questions described?
❏ Was a final list of questions included?

VII. Procedures for Collecting and Analyzing Evaluation Information

A. Methods of collecting data
   ❏ Was the time period during which data collection occurred indicated?
   ❏ Was the number of participants given for each type of data collected?
   ❏ Was the sampling method described (if applicable)?
   ❏ Were data collection techniques summarized?
   ❏ Were the sources for test scores and/or any other type of data obtained from records provided?

(Continued)

Figure 9.3 (continued)

❏ Has the reader been referred to an appendix for a specimen copy of the instrument?

B. Data analysis methods
❏ Were there separate descriptions for the quantitative and qualitative approaches used to summarize and interpret information?

VIII. Evaluation Results and Interpretation
❏ Was the reader informed that the results were organized according to each evaluation question?
❏ Was each question stated and the results explained?
❏ Were results explained clearly?
❏ Have technical concepts (e.g., formative and summative evaluation and improvement ratio) been explained clearly?
❏ Has the return rate for usable survey questionnaires been indicated?
❏ If they occurred, were any other positive or negative aspects of the program discussed?

IX. Conclusions and Recommendations
❏ Was the overall effectiveness of the program evaluated?
❏ Were the criteria used to judge overall effectiveness described?
❏ Were the strengths of the program discussed?
❏ Were conclusions drawn about the program's efficiency?

A. Have the following been indicated?
❏ Aspects of the program that should continue as they are currently being implemented
❏ Recommendations for improvement
❏ Suggestions obtained from the program staff and credited to them
❏ Suggestions offered by the evaluation team including a brief reason for each

B. If applicable:
❏ If the assessment of the program was qualified, was the context for delivering the curriculum discussed?
❏ Have steps been indicated to improve a completed (or similar) program if it were to start up in the future?
❏ Has the rationale for the team's recommendation for replacing the program been included?

X. Appendices
❏ Have specimen copies of instruments been included, each as a separate appendix with a title sheet?

PART II: MECHANICS
A. Is the information presented accurate? For example, have the following been checked?
❏ Number of participants
❏ Testing dates

❑ Titles of texts used
❑ Scheduling of classes
❑ Results of analyses

B. Has the report been proofread by the evaluation team for the following?
❑ Content
❑ Omissions
❑ Grammatical errors
❑ Typographical errors

C. Overall, does the document have a professional appearance?
❑ Has an attractive font been selected?
❑ Does the use of spacing and headings enhance readability?
❑ Have the formats for the tables been followed?
❑ Where graphics have been included, do they contribute to the presentation?
❑ Are the cover and binding appropriate for a professional document?

CHAPTER 9 HIGHLIGHTS

1.   How relevant, credible, and ultimately usable the evaluation is to stakeholders depends in large measure on the quality of the evaluation report.

2.   A format for systematically organizing the evaluation report should be followed.

3.   The report should confirm the extent to which a program is effective and also diagnose areas in which improvements are needed.

4.   The report should be respected for its excellence, fairness, and professionalism.

5.   The report should represent a viable reference from which administrators and faculty can learn.

6.   Writing the report can serve as a professional development activity.

7.   Using a checklist that addresses the contents and mechanics of a report can guide the writing of it.

NOTES

1. From their examination of the literature, Fitzpatrick et al. (2004) discuss credibility, relevance, and other factors that relate to the use of the evaluation report.

2. A feature of summative evaluation indicated by Fitzpatrick et al. (2004) is that it is used "to make decisions about the program's future or adoption" (p. 20).

3. Organizing results according to each evaluation question is recommended by Fitzpatrick et al. (2004).

4. That objectivity should be a characteristic of program assessment is consistent with reporting evaluations impartially (Fitzpatrick et al., 2004; Joint Committee on Standards, 1994).

5. The importance of fairness in evaluation reports is underscored by Fitzpatrick et al. (2004) who regard this standard as the hallmark of professionalism.

6. This checklist, in part, builds upon the works of the Joint Committee on Standards (1994) and Fitzpatrick et al. (2004). The latter authors have also created a useful checklist for writing the evaluation report.

10

Assessing the Evaluation Project

Formative and summative approaches to program evaluation can also be applied to a metaevaluation, which involves assessing the evaluation study itself (Fitzpatrick et al., 2004; Joint Committee on Standards, 1994). This chapter describes the purpose of each of these approaches and how to obtain (a) formative information to improve the operations of an evaluation currently in progress and (b) summative information to guide future program assessments.

PURPOSES OF METAEVALUATION

The formative role played in carrying out a metaevaluation involves guiding "the planning and implementation of a program evaluation" (Joint Committee on Standards, 1994, p. 185). However, "the summative role is to assess the worth and merit of a completed program evaluation" (p. 185).

Conducting both aspects of metaevaluation by the evaluation team would be a productive endeavor since these activities

> can be expected to facilitate early identification and corrections of potentially fatal flaws in a program evaluation plan, increase the likelihood that evaluation conclusions are valid, and enhance the acceptance by users and stakeholders, and . . . may increase the cost effectiveness of the program evaluation (Joint Committee on Standards, 1994, p. 186).

Figure 10.1 Monitoring the Evaluation

Phase	Task	Task Completed Successfully Yes	No	If "no," indicate action(s) needed.
1. Describing the program	Write a description of the program.			
2. Providing direction for the evaluation	Formulate goal-related evaluation questions.			
	Distribute program goals, goal-related, and generic evaluation questions to stakeholders.			
	Ask stakeholders for suggestions for other questions.			
	Stakeholders and evaluation team judge which questions are addressed.			
	Obtain consensus between evaluation team and stakeholders on final choice of questions.			
Before collecting any data, complete the Evaluation Plan (Figure 7.6 in Chapter 7).				

148

3. Obtaining information to answer evaluation questions				
Decide whether to use a sample or entire population of students.				
Use sampling (if applicable).				
Decide if a control group should be used.				
Select data collection methods for each evaluation question: • survey questionnaire(s) • interview questions • follow-up questions • obtaining process information • observations				
Adhere to ethical data collection methods.				

(Continued)

Figure 10.1 (continued)

| Phase | Task | Task Completed Successfully | | If "no," indicate action(s) needed. |
		Yes	No	
4. Analyzing data to assess the program's impact	Appropriate for the evaluation question: • complete analysis of quantitative data • complete analysis of qualitative data			
5 Evaluating the program's effectiveness and offering recommendations for its future	Draw conclusions about the program's effectiveness and efficiency.			
	Provide recommendations for the program's future.			
6. Writing the evaluation report	Present draft version of report document to stakeholders for feedback.			
	Make necessary revisions for the final report.			

150

FORMATIVE METAEVALUATION

Fitzpatrick et al. (2004) indicate the importance of monitoring the evaluation while it is in progress so that revisions can be made in light of any problems encountered. This activity is consistent with the formative aspect of program evaluation. In this regard, the evaluation team should address the question of whether the project tasks are being completed as planned (Fitzpatrick et al., 2004). If they are not, asking what improvements or changes are needed to remedy the situation should be elicited. Such an inquiry should be made at each phase of the evaluation project. The form shown in Figure 10.1 can be used to facilitate this task.

Applying a formative approach to identifying and improving aspects concerning the process of program evaluation should also extend to how well the evaluation team is functioning. For this purpose, its members would respond to and discuss questions about the effectiveness and efficiency of the team process. This can be done at a meeting with a view toward exploring actions that can be taken to improve any aspect of how the team is operating. Figure 10.2 lists examples of formative questions that can be raised.

The types of questions in Figure 10.2 are compatible with the spirit of a collaborative learning culture. From this perspective, they could facilitate introspection among the group, thereby leading to personal and professional growth.

Figure 10.2   Judging Evaluation Team Functioning: Questions for Formative Assessment of Evaluation Team Process

- As a team, are we accomplishing our tasks well?
- Are we on schedule according to the Evaluation Time Log (Figure 7.6 in Chapter 7)?
- Are our meetings efficient with little or no wasted time?
- Do you look forward to attending our meetings?
- Do you have any recommendations for improving the team process?

SUMMATIVE METAEVALUATION

The questionnaire in Figure 10.3 can be used by individual members of the evaluation team in their overall assessment of the project after it has been completed.[1] It should be answered anonymously. Items can also be added, modified, or omitted.

The instrument taps opinions regarding the quality of the evaluation project and its potential influence on the organization (items 1–12), and the perceived effects on the individual team member by having participated in this endeavor (items 13–17). The rationale for including organizational and individual dimensions draws from the separate models of Kirkhart and Henry and Mark concerning the influence, that is, the effects produced by a program assessment as treated in Fitzpatrick et al. (2004). These models, as discussed below, provide perspectives applicable to a summative program evaluation since the more positive the perceived effects or consequences of an assessment, the greater the likelihood that the overall judgment of the project's usefulness will be favorable.

Evaluations can influence practice because of the *results* and/or the *process* involved in carrying out the assessment. Influence impacts two levels—the organization and individual faculty members. Regarding the former, influence would be manifested by the decisions made about the program's future. Should the program continue in its present form, be modified, or be replaced is an organizational issue since actions growing out of this decision could affect the school's subsequent performance.

With respect to the process dimension of influence, participation in an assessment project by an evaluation team member could lead to a greater appreciation of the benefits derived from determining the worth of a program which could find expression in changes made by the teacher in his or her classroom. Put another way, such participation provides experiences conducive to growth. It can do this since functioning in an evaluator's role provides opportunities for proactive planning how project tasks can be completed efficiently as well as for being reflective in drawing conclusions and making recommendations. The interplay of both cognitive processes, along with gaining knowledge of assessment principles and techniques, can enhance instructional competencies. Moreover, the influence of the evaluation can extend to faculty members outside of the team who can see how aspects of the report could be applied to their own teaching.

The questionnaire in Figure 10.3 links four dimensions of summative metaevaluation. In this regard, the items measure judgment in terms that has the respondent consider the effects on an *organization* produced by the *results* of an evaluation and the effects on an *individual* by having participated in the *process* of carrying out the assessment.

To lend more objectivity to the metaevaluation, perspectives from the stakeholders who were involved from the beginning of the evaluation project should be obtained.[2, 3] For this purpose, items 1 through 10 can be used as a separate questionnaire (see Figure 10.4). These tap opinions of this group as well as those of the team members concerning the quality and potential effects of the evaluation. Thus the items that reflect the professional growth dimension concerning the value of the project for individual team members, are not included.

Figure 10.3   Judging the Program Evaluation Project—Team Members

Evaluation Project Assessment Questionnaire

The following items* concern the work of the evaluation team as well as your role in the evaluation project. Your responses will provide useful information for the next team.

Directions

Please place a check in the box that best indicates the extent to which you agree with each statement. Any comments that explain your opinion will be very helpful.

1. The evaluation report reflects that a systematic evaluation was conducted.

Strongly agree	Agree	Undecided	Disagree	Strongly disagree
❑	❑	❑	❑	❑

Comment:_____

_____

_____

2. The evaluation report reflects that a comprehensive evaluation was conducted.

Strongly agree	Agree	Undecided	Disagree	Strongly disagree
❑	❑	❑	❑	❑

Comment:_____

_____

_____

3. Relevant data were collected to address the evaluation questions.

Strongly agree	Agree	Undecided	Disagree	Strongly disagree
❑	❑	❑	❑	❑

Comment:_____

_____

_____

4. The components of the report were covered in sufficient depth.

Strongly agree	Agree	Undecided	Disagree	Strongly disagree
❑	❑	❑	❑	❑

Comment:_____

_____

_____

5. Results of the evaluation were clearly presented.

Strongly agree	Agree	Undecided	Disagree	Strongly disagree
❑	❑	❑	❑	❑

Comment:_____

_____

_____

(Continued)

Figure 10.3   (continued)

6. From the evidence collected, the conclusions drawn were justified.

Strongly agree	Agree	Undecided	Disagree	Strongly disagree
❑	❑	❑	❑	❑

Comment:_____

_____

_____

7. From the results of the data analyzed, the recommendations given were justified.

Strongly agree	Agree	Undecided	Disagree	Strongly disagree
❑	❑	❑	❑	❑

Comment:_____

_____

_____

8. The report was disseminated in enough time to make decisions about its recommendations.

Strongly agree	Agree	Undecided	Disagree	Strongly disagree
❑	❑	❑	❑	❑

Comment:_____

_____

_____

9. The report will be useful to the staff delivering the program.

Strongly agree	Agree	Undecided	Disagree	Strongly disagree
❑	❑	❑	❑	❑

Comment:_____

_____

_____

10. The report reflects professional quality.

Strongly agree	Agree	Undecided	Disagree	Strongly disagree
❑	❑	❑	❑	❑

Comment:_____

_____

_____

11. Plans for conducting the evaluation were sound.

Strongly agree	Agree	Undecided	Disagree	Strongly disagree
❏	❏	❏	❏	❏

Comment:_____

_____

_____

12. Procedures were carried out as planned.

Strongly agree	Agree	Undecided	Disagree	Strongly disagree
❏	❏	❏	❏	❏

Comment:_____

_____

_____

13. When it was recommended that a curriculum be modified, feasible plans to implement changes were made that involved the principal and program staff.

Strongly agree	Agree	Undecided	Disagree	Strongly disagree
❏	❏	❏	❏	❏

Comment:_____

_____

_____

14. I have gained knowledge about evaluation that will be useful in assessing my own students' learning.

Strongly agree	Agree	Undecided	Disagree	Strongly disagree
❏	❏	❏	❏	❏

Comment:_____

_____

_____

15. I have gained knowledge about factors that can affect the delivery of a program.

Strongly agree	Agree	Undecided	Disagree	Strongly disagree
❏	❏	❏	❏	❏

Comment:_____

_____

_____

(Continued)

Figure 10.3   (continued)

16. I have gained insights about the elements that constitute an effective program.

Strongly agree	Agree	Undecided	Disagree	Strongly disagree
❑	❑	❑	❑	❑

Comment:_____

_____

_____

17. Participation in the evaluation project was worth the time and effort since the results and recommendations can help improve student achievement.

Strongly agree	Agree	Undecided	Disagree	Strongly disagree
❑	❑	❑	❑	❑

Comment:_____

_____

_____

18. My participation in the evaluation project enhanced my growth as a professional.

Strongly agree	Agree	Undecided	Disagree	Strongly disagree
❑	❑	❑	❑	❑

Comment:_____

_____

_____

If you have any recommendations for improving the evaluation report, please indicate these below.

_____

_____

_____

If you have any recommendations for improving the process of conducting an evaluation for the next evaluation team, please indicate these below.

_____

_____

_____

Thank you for your input.

* Items 1 through 12 are based on material found in Fitzpatrick et al. (2004) and the Joint Committee on Standards (1994).

Figure 10.4   Judging the Program Evaluation Project—Stakeholders

Evaluation Project Assessment Questionnaire

The following items concern the work of the evaluation team. Your responses will provide useful information for the next team.

Directions

Please place a check in the box that best indicates the extent to which you agree with each statement. Any comments that explain your opinion will be very helpful.

1. The evaluation report reflects that a systematic evaluation was conducted.

Strongly agree	Agree	Undecided	Disagree	Strongly disagree
❑	❑	❑	❑	❑

Comment:_____

_____

_____

2. The evaluation report reflects that a comprehensive evaluation was conducted.

Strongly agree	Agree	Undecided	Disagree	Strongly disagree
❑	❑	❑	❑	❑

Comment:_____

_____

_____

3. Relevant data were collected to address the evaluation questions.

Strongly agree	Agree	Undecided	Disagree	Strongly disagree
❑	❑	❑	❑	❑

Comment:_____

_____

_____

4. The components of the report were covered in sufficient depth.

Strongly agree	Agree	Undecided	Disagree	Strongly disagree
❑	❑	❑	❑	❑

Comment:_____

_____

_____

(Continued)

Figure 10.4   (continued)

5. Results of the evaluation were clearly presented.

Strongly agree	Agree	Undecided	Disagree	Strongly disagree
❏	❏	❏	❏	❏

Comment:_____

_____

_____

6. From the evidence collected, the conclusions drawn were justified.

Strongly agree	Agree	Undecided	Disagree	Strongly disagree
❏	❏	❏	❏	❏

Comment:_____

_____

_____

7. From the results of the data analyzed, the recommendations given were justified.

Strongly agree	Agree	Undecided	Disagree	Strongly disagree
❏	❏	❏	❏	❏

Comment:_____

_____

_____

8. The report was disseminated in enough time to make decisions about its recommendations.

Strongly agree	Agree	Undecided	Disagree	Strongly disagree
❏	❏	❏	❏	❏

Comment:_____

_____

_____

9. The report will be useful to the staff delivering the program.

Strongly agree	Agree	Undecided	Disagree	Strongly disagree
❏	❏	❏	❏	❏

Comment:_____

_____

_____

10. The report reflects professional quality.

Strongly agree	Agree	Undecided	Disagree	Strongly disagree
❑	❑	❑	❑	❑

Comment:_____

_____

_____

If you have any recommendations for improving the evaluation report, please indicate these below.

_____

_____

_____

If you have any recommendations for improving the process of conducting an evaluation for the next evaluation team, please indicate these below.

_____

_____

_____

Thank you for your input.

Analyzing Metaevaluation Data

Responses to the questionnaire can be analyzed on an item-by-item basis. This approach has the advantage of disclosing information on specific aspects of the program evaluation that were seen as effective and identifying any areas that should be improved in a future assessment.

Using the Likert scale accompanying each statement, choices are weighted in descending order from "5" to "1" for the "Strongly agree" to "Strongly disagree" options. Item means can next be calculated by adding the scores for all of the team members and then dividing the total by the number of individuals in the group. For example, if there were five team members and their total was 22, the mean would be 4.4.

To obtain an average judgment of the entire metaevaluation, all of the item means are added and this figure is divided by the total number of items used. A conclusion stated in qualitative terms should then be made. As an example, if the overall mean was 4.2 it can then be stated that the quality of the metaevaluation was rated rather favorably by the team members.

Item and overall analyses can also be made for the questionnaires containing the same items given to the team and stakeholders. Both groups can then be compared as shown in Figure 10.5. Where there is a noticeable difference in means (.5 and above) the comments accompanying each item may provide clues as to the discrepancy.

Figure 10.5   A Comparison of Team Members and Stakehoders on Measures of Summative Metaevaluation

Item	Team mean	Stakeholder mean	Difference
1. The evaluation report reflects that a systematic evaluation was conducted.	x.xx	x.xx	x.xx
2. The evaluation report reflects that a comprehensive evaluation was conducted.	x.xx	x.xx	x.xx
3. Relevant data were collected to address the evaluation questions.	x.xx	x.xx	x.xx
4. The components of the report were covered in sufficient depth.	x.xx	x.xx	x.xx
5. Results of the evaluation were clearly presented.	x.xx	x.xx	x.xx
6. From the evidence collected, the conclusions drawn were justified.	x.xx	x.xx	x.xx
7. From the results of the data analyzed, the recommendations given were justified.	x.xx	x.xx	x.xx
8. The report was disseminated in enough time to make decisions about its recommendations.	x.xx	x.xx	x.xx
9. The report will be useful to the staff delivering the program.	x.xx	x.xx	x.xx
10. The report reflects professional quality.	x.xx	x.xx	x.xx
Overall mean	x.xx	x.xx	x.xx

As a further note, metaevaluation results should be summarized in a report to the principal submitted by the team. This information can be helpful to the succeeding team.

A CONCLUDING NOTE

Metaevaluation and reflective practice are congruous. Thus carrying out each phase of metaevaluation requires reflection. This occurs at the planning, process, and terminal stages of the study. As with any endeavor to improve a situation, current efforts should be analyzed, alternatives weighed, a plan implemented, and its effects assessed. In this regard, metaevaluation strengthens the link between the process of assessing a program and its development since sound evaluation discloses where and how future instruction should be concentrated. Furthermore, conducting formative and summative metaevaluations parallels the confirming and diagnostic functions of program evaluation.[4] Concerning the former, a sound program assessment can affirm the work of the team. The value of the diagnostic aspect is reflected in any feedback that indicates where or how an evaluation project can be improved.

CHAPTER 10 HIGHLIGHTS

1.   Formative and summative approaches can be applied to assessing the evaluation study itself. These activities constitute a metaevaluation.

2.   Formative information should be obtained at each phase of the evaluation. This task can be facilitated by using a checklist to make any needed modifications to complete the tasks involved in the project.

3.   Questions can be raised to determine the effectiveness and efficiency of the team process.

4.   From a summative perspective, questionnaires answered by the team members and stakeholders to measure their overall assessment of the completed evaluation project should be helpful to succeeding teams.

5.   Metaevaluation and reflective practice are congruous since reflection is required when carrying out this type of evaluation.

6.   Metaevaluation strengthens the link between the process of assessing a program and its development.

7.   Conducting formative and summative metaevaluations parallels the confirming and diagnostic functions of program evaluation.

NOTES

1. In their discussion of metaevaluation, Fitzpatrick et al. (2004) include a sample checklist that they indicate can be used for judging evaluation reports and designs based on the work of The Joint Committee on Standards.

2. Having stakeholders also provide metaevaluation data is in keeping with that recommended by Fitzpatrick et al. (2004).

3. While they function as evaluators, the team members would also be stakeholders in that they would have a stake in the success of any program in their school.

4. The diagnostic purpose of program evaluation is indicated in Fitzpatrick et al. (2004).

11

Revisiting the Principal's
Leadership Role in Program
Evaluation

This chapter expands on the basic premise of the book: conducting a program evaluation that leads to higher student achievement depends, in the final analysis, on what the principal has done to promote and support the various phases of the project. An instrument for a principal's self-assessment is also included to raise into saliency leadership factors to help ensure that the evaluation process makes a meaningful impact on the organization. The chapter concludes with a perspective on winning that views standardized testing as a welcome opportunity to demonstrate effective teaching and learning.

THE MULTIDIMENSIONAL RESPONSIBILITIES OF THE PRINCIPAL IN PROGRAM EVALUATION

This book has described a systematic and comprehensive approach for conducting a program evaluation. However, the potential of an assessment study for improving student achievement will not be realized without the leadership initiatives[1] and follow-through actions a principal can take to help ensure the project's success. In this regard, DeRoche (1987) argues that "a principal's attitudes and procedures can make the evaluation program an enlightening, interesting, exciting venture or one that is frustrating, based on fear, and viewed negatively by those involved" (p. 6).

Considering this perspective, specific implications of a principal's active intervention in various phases of an assessment project are indicated next.

When a principal

- promotes the need for an evaluation team, supports its activities, and provides a place for it as a regular part of the school organization, this speaks to the importance of assessing programs as a means of improving student achievement;
- makes her- or himself available to assist the team by handling administrative type tasks if called upon, or providing knowledge of the evaluation process when needed, this facilitates the completion of the project;
- acts on the recommendation of the evaluation team at the close of the study, this helps ensure that its report will be used to enhance program delivery; and
- recognizes the team's accomplishments as well as those of the program staff and their students, this contributes to feelings of satisfaction and heightened motivation.

The principal's involvement in an evaluation project is driven by the attitudes he or she has toward this endeavor. Encouraging attitudes find expression when the administrator communicates the benefits that can occur as a result of the faculty conducting its own program assessments.

ATTITUDES OF PRINCIPALS TOWARD ASSESSING PROGRAMS

Standardized tests provide one gauge for measuring organizational performance. However, as indicated earlier, the results they yield should not be the only means for judging a program's effectiveness (Fitzpatrick et al., 2004; Joint Committee on Standards, 1994). Rather, this determination should be based on a number of indicators since these provide additional evidence to corroborate the extent to which a program is successful. Standardized tests obviously would not be used to judge student achievement where there are a variety of curricular goals (e.g., interpersonal relations, community service, and creativity in science and social studies projects). Therefore, these types of outcomes should also be assessed to determine the overall worth of a program if they reflect its goals. Put another way, if a goal is important enough to include in a program, the extent to which it has been achieved must be considered when drawing conclusions about the program's impact.

With this in mind, a principal should convey to the staff the value of assessing program outcomes and processes in explicit terms. The following are recommended points to cover.

Evaluating Program Outcomes in a Comprehensive Way Is Worthwhile

It provides an overall perspective on the extent to which students are progressing on each curriculum goal. As such, when evidence of success is found, this confirms for members of a learning organization where efforts have been effective. If assessment discloses results that are less than satisfactory, then this information can help focus attention on areas needing remediation.

Determining a Program's Success Solely on the Results of Standardized Tests Is Not Evaluation, It Is Measurement—Professional Judgment Is Not Involved

Test scores can have the effect of driving the curriculum because they provide a narrow focus on what is being assessed (Joint Committee on Standards, 1994). This effect can detract educators from concentrating on other important goals besides those that the tests measure.

Using Valid Indicators of Program Effectiveness Helps Gauge the Level of Professional Performance

Since each school is accountable for student achievement, it is essential for the staff, as professionals, to use valid indicators to judge their work systematically and comprehensively. Furthermore, program evaluation should also be included as part of the curriculum development process.

Reflecting on Practice Suggests Areas in Need of Improvement

The process of assessing programs contributes to professional development. Since this process requires reflecting on practices, it serves as a stimulus for thought on how to improve curriculum delivery. Thus such reflection involves a level of introspection, both individual and group, that can lead to promising strategies in areas of needed growth for educators.

BEYOND THE TECHNICAL

Program evaluation should be considered a tool that can be applied to enhance organizational outcomes. As such, it yields information that leads to decisions regarding directions for improving curricular activities that can elevate student achievement. This information also suggests areas for the principal to focus on in exercising instructional leadership. (One source for this data is the needs assessment completed by program staff that was presented in Chapter 7.)

Undergirding what any curriculum can accomplish are inner qualities of a principal's leadership such as resolve (Jason, 1998), conviction, confidence, passion, optimism, and spirit. These are intangible, yet powerful, factors that drive endeavors because they galvanize followers.

These factors provide the emotional fuel that propels an organization since they inspire followers as well as leaders themselves to take actions toward higher levels of accomplishment. Such factors work their influence because people function better in an environment where their energies are not dissipated by negativism, worry, and/or pessimism. Positive emotions that are reflected in a leader's demeanor and behavior communicate the promise of a better quality of work life.[2] In this regard, people in an organization become less daunted by difficulties because they see that their leader is at least trying to remedy them and can possibly do so. In fact, "difficulties" cast in a different light and perceived as challenges are motivating. It is in the human psyche to rise to a challenge, and this tropism can be channeled toward eliminating or minimizing barriers that hamper better student achievement.

The Potential of Schoolwide Leadership

While this chapter has focused on the role of the principal in program evaluation, no one person should be thought of as the fountainhead for leadership actions. This is consistent with Schmoker (1999) who indicates that only rare principals can create higher achievement by themselves. He points out that the potent combination of principal and teacher leadership increases the chance for instructional changes to occur. Schmoker further maintains that any of the staff can exercise leadership by assuming responsibility for the organization's success by influencing other members.

Empirical support for Schmoker's (1999) position is the citing by Duke (2006) of studies published between 1999 and 2004 in which low-performing schools made turnarounds. He reports that one of the key elements for their success in raising "academic achievement to impressive levels" (p. 730) is the leadership of principals and teacher leaders whose actions "set the tone for the school improvement process" (p. 730). In addition to leadership, among other factors that Duke reports as being related to increased student achievement in these schools are also features of site-based program evaluation. These involve teacher collaboration, data-based decision making, and an organizational structure that includes teams. The latter is aligned with what was highlighted earlier with respect to having an evaluation team in place to conduct program assessments as an ongoing function of the school as a learning organization.

Against this background, principals should communicate the potential that leadership initiatives taken by all staff members have in improving school performance. When this mentality is pervasive, student achievement should be raised since the collective weight of experience, expertise, and commitment is brought to bear on solving problems—a characteristic of learning organizations.[3] Thus consistent with DuFour and Eaker (1992), when personnel in a school perceive of themselves as learners as well as professionals, they become more willing to experiment with and modify programs as needed. In this context, these authors refer to Barth's concept of a "community of learners" in which commitment to experimentation and school improvement are linked. Moreover, in keeping with what Barth advocates, members of a learning organization embrace the belief that learning can be exciting and rewarding, not only for their students but for themselves as well.

Characteristic of this setting is "learner-centered leadership," a competence of educational leaders posited by Roberts (2000). She maintains that "in such a culture, all people in the system are seen as learners and act as learners" (p. 417). As with any dimension of personal and professional development, what a principal can learn through participation in an evaluation project would be facilitated by being introspective about his or her leadership in this endeavor. An instrument designed to facilitate this process of reflection is described next.

PRINCIPAL'S SELF-ASSESSMENT

With respect to the principal's role in program evaluation, the instrument in Figure 11.1 should be useful in guiding her or his actions in the assessment process. Note that most questions can be answered during the course of the evaluation project, and any changes in actions can be made to facilitate the work of the evaluation team. Principals can also reflect on their role after an evaluation has been completed, and, as members of a learning organization, they can apply what they have gained through this self-assessment for future projects.

Figure 11.1   Self-Ratings of the Principal's Role in Program Evaluation

Principal Self-Assessment Questionnaire: Program Evaluation Project

	Yes	Somewhat	No
1. Have I promoted a sufficient need for program evaluation?*	❏	❏	❏

Specific action to take:

_____

_____

| 2. Have I followed systematic procedures when forming the evaluation team? | ❏ | ❏ | ❏ |

Specific action to take:

_____

_____

| 3. Have I provided resources to facilitate the completion of the evaluation project?* | ❏ | ❏ | ❏ |

Specific action to take:

_____

_____

| 4. Have I shown enthusiasm for the evaluation project? | | | |
Specific action to take: | ❏ | ❏ | ❏ |

_____

_____

| 5. Have I been available for assistance, if needed, by the evaluation team? | ❏ | ❏ | ❏ |

Specific action to take:

_____

_____

| 6. Have I encouraged the evaluation team? | ❏ | ❏ | ❏ |
Specific action to take:

_____

_____

| 7. Have I formally and informally recognized accomplishments of the program faculty being evaluated?** | ❏ | ❏ | ❏ |

Specific action to take:

_____

_____

8. Have I formally and informally recognized accomplishments of the students in the program being evaluated?**   ❏   ❏   ❏

   Specific action to take:

   _____

   _____

9. Have I formally and informally recognized accomplishments of the evaluation team?**   ❏   ❏   ❏

   Specific action to take:

   _____

   _____

10. Have I followed up on recommendations given in the evaluation report?   ❏   ❏   ❏

    Specific action to take:

    _____

    _____

---

* Items 1 and 3 are based on recommendations for the principal in the evaluation process indicated by DeRoche (1987).

** Although not in the context of conducting program evaluations, Schmoker (1999) discusses the importance of leaders giving public and private recognition for school improvement. This is reflected in items 7, 8, and 9.

A CONCLUDING NOTE

At the beginning of this work, it was stated that this book was about winning. But this perspective goes beyond the traditional notion that if there are winners, there must also be losers. Instead, consider the potential that winning can have if self-improvement were emphasized. This outlook can lead to students achieving at higher levels than would be the case if the focus were on informing them about how they stood relative to a grade level standard. Athletes know well the value of judging their performance in terms of how they are doing now as compared to what they have demonstrated earlier. When they experience a "personal best," this carries with it feelings of excitement and satisfaction as well as increased motivation to exceed this level. This experience should also occur in an academic setting. In this regard, according to Schmoker (1999), teachers should discuss with their students on a regular basis the progress they are making and also recognize improvement and effort. Based on this point, the goal would be to have students develop enough confidence in their abilities so that they feel they can earn satisfactory or even excellent scores on standardized tests.

This belief, coupled with having both sufficient academic preparation and test-taking skills, should lessen stress and debilitating anxiety that can result from pressure to do well. Pressure to perform in any arena can in the long run be counterproductive, especially if it exceeds a tolerable point. Thus ironically, exhortations to achieve are not likely to have their intended effect. Exacerbating this is students and teachers knowing the consequences of substandard results. This environment makes a prospective test event, as well as the testing situation itself, too intensive and detracts from making school a satisfying and enjoyable experience. To counteract this requires a diametrically different view of standardized testing, from that of a threat to an event that provides a good opportunity to demonstrate how successful students and teachers have been in performing their roles.[4] A positive perception of an upcoming challenging situation is liberating and can help minimize the deleterious effects that excess worrying has on preparing for and taking tests.

Considering testing as an opportunity is congruous with conducting program evaluation with a view toward self-improvement, not only for students but for faculty as well. When students meet or exceed standards in various areas of knowledge and skills, this adds information to the outcomes dimension of evaluation. However, where their performance is less than satisfactory, such results, as stated earlier, will suggest directions for improving the process of delivering the curriculum. Assessing this process fits within the framework of personal mastery that for Senge (1990) is pivotal in a learning organization. Personal mastery is winning on a personal level. In terms of school performance, this perspective is practical because it extends to helping students recognize where they need to improve. It enables the program staff to be more efficient in remedying aspects of the curriculum and its delivery because such efforts can then be concentrated on where there is greater need. Therefore, focusing on deficiencies which performers in various disciplines accept as a given, is essential not only for improvement, but for achieving excellence as well.

Consistent with Senge (1990), the concept of continuous self-improvement is inherent in the thrust of a learning organization. By adopting the values of such an organization, school personnel will more readily embrace the promise of lessons that can be learned from program evaluation projects. From this perspective, when carrying out these assessments regularly determines that a particular curriculum is doing its "job" well by enhancing instruction, it provides teachers with a winning edge. This would be leverage that, congruent with a systems mentality of a learning organization, can be instrumental in the improvement process.

In bringing this book to a close, it seems appropriate to point out that individuals achieve more when they accept a message from those they believe in that conveys confidence, support, and optimism about their future performance.[5] Therefore, administrators and staff should communicate the following sentiment: Bring on the tests. Our students are ready for them, and they will succeed!

Conducting program evaluations by local school personnel will help strengthen this conviction by guiding actions aimed at preparing students to do well not only on standardized tests but also on other indicators of effectiveness. In this context, the professional knowledge gained by educators from assessing their work can provide the momentum to raise achievement to new heights.

CHAPTER 11 HIGHLIGHTS

1. The potential of a program evaluation for improving student achievement will not be realized without the principal's leadership initiatives and follow-through actions.

2. The principal's involvement in an evaluation project is driven by the attitudes he or she has towards this endeavor.

3. A principal should convey to the staff the value of assessing program outcomes and processes in explicit terms.

4. Undergirding what any curriculum can accomplish are inner qualities of a principal's leadership.

5. Leadership initiatives taken by all staff members can improve the performance of the school as a learning organization.

6. Self-assessment by principals regarding their role in program evaluation should be useful in guiding their actions in the assessment process.

7. If winning were emphasized from a self-improvement perspective, this could lead to higher levels of student achievement.

8. Standardized testing should be viewed not as a threat, but as an opportunity to demonstrate successful teaching and learning.

9. A positive perception toward testing is liberating and can help minimize the effects of worry on preparing for and taking tests.

10. Viewing winning as personal mastery helps students recognize what they need to improve and enables program staff to concentrate their efforts on where there is greater need.

11. Administrators and staff should communicate the sentiment that their students are ready for testing and will be successful.

NOTES

1. While his book encompasses both program and personnel evaluation, De-Roche (1987) identifies the principal's formulation of evaluation plans and procedures as a leadership activity.

2. Based on Wheatley's book *Leadership and the New Science*, published in 1994, Schmoker (1999) discusses how destructive thoughts that detract from improving a workplace can be replaced by school leaders who promote a positive, productive, and purposeful culture by celebrating accomplishments.

3. The link between collective intelligence and school improvement is underscored by Schmoker (1999).

4. DeRoche (1987) indicates that the process of evaluation should help determine the success of teaching and learning.

5. Schmoker (1999) calls attention to the need for leaders to communicate confidence regarding what can be achieved by the organization.

A Miniguide for the
Evaluation Team Leader

Introduction

In coordinating the multifaceted and numerous tasks involved in evaluating a program, the role of the team leader encompasses that of serving as a facilitator who has a *basic knowledge* about the assessment process. As an aid in acquiring such knowledge, it is recommended that you first get an overview of what a program evaluation entails by reading Chapters 7 through 10 in a general way. Then focus on "digesting" the material involved in carrying out tasks related to the phase(s) the team will be working on. In this regard, reflect on how the tasks should be handled. Consider possible problems or obstacles that could hamper completing an activity and how these situations could be prevented or minimized. Such thinking should enhance the leadership and managerial dimensions involved in serving as a facilitator.

In Support of the Team Leader's Role

By demonstrating knowledge of the assessment process throughout the course of the evaluation, a leader builds confidence that the project is in capable hands. This perception serves to minimize the opportunity for frustration if it appears that the team is "spinning its wheels" because it does not have a sense of direction. This situation can be prevented by the leader being proactive and communicating an understanding of what needs to be accomplished. This combination should help keep the work on track and put the leader in a better position to respond to questions posed by team members, the staff delivering the program, and other stakeholders. Finally, as was stated earlier, program evaluation is a professional development activity. The team leader has a pivotal role in this endeavor as he or she, in collaboration with the team, gains worthwhile experience in systematically carrying out the steps of the evaluation process.

Organization of the Guide

This section synthesizes the steps to follow in conducting a program evaluation. Its contents are in the form of a checklist that covers Phases 1 through 6 as described in Chapters 7 and 8 as well as writing the evaluation report (Chapter 9) and carrying out a metaevaluation (Chapter 10). The guide also covers the beginning of the assessment project when the team first meets and ends with topics for the leader to discuss with respect to conducting an experiment with a modified curriculum. The numbers shown in parenthesis after a task refer to the page(s) and figure(s) in which the material is found. This makes it more convenient for the leader when planning and explaining the various actions needed by the team.

Boxes are provided as a means of checking whether the activities have been completed or are still in progress. The guidelines are structured according to the major areas to be covered and by addressing the various areas involved in the assessment activities help ensure the success of the evaluation project.

TASK

Prepare for the first meeting:

COMPLETED

❏   Review suggestions for the team leader concerning how to conduct meetings. (56–57; Fig. 5.3, 56)

At the first meeting explain the following:

❏   How program evaluation contributes to school improvement. (1–2; Fig. 1.1, 2)

❏   Benefits of site-based program evaluation. (3–4; Fig. 1.3, 4)

❏   Present overview of the evaluation project. (Fig. 5.4, 57)

❏   How the program evaluation process would be systematic by referring to the phases of the project and comprehensive by indicating the different types of data that can be collected. (64–65, 77, 89, 111)

❏   Remarks about the work of the team. (54; Fig. 5.2, 55)

❏   Difference between summative and formative evaluation. (5–7; Fig. 1.4, 6)

❏   The cyclical process of improving a curriculum through program evaluation. (7; Fig. 1.5, 8)

Topics to cover are subsumed under each section below.

Phase 1: *Describing the Program*

❏ Explain why a program should be evaluated after a minimum of one year. (77)

❏ Explain the purpose of writing a program description and discuss the parts that compose it. (78–80)

Phase 2: *Providing Direction for the Evaluation*

Explain the following:

❏ The purpose of evaluation questions. (80–81)

❏ The difference between outcome and generic questions. (80–83)

The steps involved in carrying out Phase 2:

❏ Formulate evaluation questions. (81–83)

❏ Present the questions to stakeholders. (83–84; Fig. 7.1, 85)

❏ Explain to stakeholders how the evaluation would be systematic and comprehensive. (64–65, 77, 89, 111)

❏ Generate other possible outcome questions. (84)

❏ Assess outcome questions. (84)

❏ Obtain consensus between stakeholders and the evaluation team on the final choice of questions to be used. (84, 86)

❏ How evaluation questions facilitate organizing assessment results. (86)

Phase 3: *Obtaining Information to Answer Evaluation Questions*

The following aspects are covered:

❏ Determining if a control group is available to serve as a basis of comparison. (86)

❏ Using a sample. (86–87)

❏ Selecting classes randomly. (88)

❏ Selecting focus groups. (88–89)

❏ Data collection methods. (89)

❏ Judging test validity and reliability and informing teachers participating in the study about how to meet these criteria. (65–71; Fig. 6.2, 67; Fig. 6.3, 68)

❏ Obtaining opinions from stakeholder groups. (89–90)

❏ Using available (or developing new) questionnaires to measure student attitudes. (90)

❏ Connecting interview questions and survey questionnaires. (90–91)

❏ Illustrating the use of Likert scales for questionnaires given to parents and students. (91)

❏ Why conduct interviews? (92)

❐   Interviewing parents. (92)
❐   The value of follow-up questions. (93)
❐   Obtaining formative information by the use of a needs assessment questionnaire. (93; 99; Fig. 7.3, 94–99)
❐   Conducting classroom observations. (100; Fig. 7.4, 100; Fig. 7.5, 101–103)

❐   Completing the Evaluation Plan. (103–104; Fig. 7.6, 104)
❐   Completing the Evaluation Time Log. (104; Fig. 7.7, 105)
❐   Ethical aspects of program evaluation. (105–106)
❐   Review of guidelines for collecting evaluation data. (106–107)

Phase 4: *Analyzing Data to Assess a Program's Impact*

Explain the following:
❐   Practical significance. (112–113)
❐   Why percentages should be used in analyzing data. (113)
❐   Measuring improvement. (114–116; Fig. 8.1, 114; Fig. 8.2, 116)
❐   Use of crossbreak tables. (116–118; Fig. 8.3, 117; Fig. 8.4, 118)
❐   Disaggregating data to determine the effects of a program on specific groups. (119–120; Fig. 8.5, 119; Fig. 8.6, 121)
❐   Use of report card grades as an outcome variable. (121; Fig. 8.7, 122)
❐   Analyzing observational data. (122; 124; Fig. 8.8, 123; Fig. 8.9, 124; Fig. 8.10, 125)
❐   Analyzing attitudinal data. (126–127; Fig. 8.11, 126)
❐   Using graphs to display results. (127; Fig. 8.12, 128; Fig. 8.13, 129)
❐   Analyzing qualitative data. (129–130)

Phase 5: *Evaluating the Program's Effectiveness and Efficiency and Offering Recommendations for its Future*

Explain the following:
❐   Considering the program's context. (131)
❐   Considering the program's efficiency. (131–132)
❐   Examining the evidence obtained by addressing the evaluation questions to support the team's judgment and recommendations. (132; Fig. 8.14, 133–134)

Phase 6: *Writing the Evaluation Report*

❐   Use of draft version to elicit feedback from stakeholders. (132, 135)
❐   Format for the report. (137–139; Fig. 9.1, 138; Fig. 9.2, 138)

Metaevaluation

❑   Formative approach to identify where and how the
         evaluation project can be improved while it is in
         progress. (151; Fig. 10.1, 148–150; Fig. 10.2, 151)
❑   Summative approach to provide an overall
         assessment of the evaluation project after it has
         been completed. (151–152; Fig. 10.3, 153–156;
         Fig. 10.4, 157–159)
❑   Submitting a report to the principal written by the team
         based on an analysis of summative metaevaluation data.
         (159–160)

The Team's Role in the Experimental Process

Based on the evaluation report, if it was decided to make changes in the curriculum and/or its delivery, consistent with the approach advocated in this book an experiment would next be implemented to determine the effectiveness of the recommended modifications. For this project, the team should meet with the teachers involved in the experiment to plan how the study will be conducted. Depending on the time in the school year that the evaluation report is completed, the team may be able to hold preliminary discussions with the program staff and other teachers if a control group is involved. However in completing its work, the team should still meet with the teachers at the beginning of the experiment, even if it is in the following school year, to discuss not only procedures to be carried out, but also the concepts and principles associated with this type of research. Obtaining consensus on how to implement the study can help ensure that a more credible experiment is conducted.

The following list contains aspects of experimental methodology to be discussed by the leader initially with the team and later with the teachers involved.

Planning an Experiment to Determine the Effectiveness of Changes Made After a Program Has Been Evaluated

❑   Experimental approach to program evaluation. (24–25;
         Fig. 3.1, 25)
❑   Concepts of internal validity and confounding. (26;
         Fig. 4.1, 37)
❑   Factors that threaten internal validity. (26–30)
❑   Building control into an experiment. (36)
❑   Planning an experiment to control extraneous variables.
         (36)
❑   Random assignment. (37–39; Fig. 4.2, 38)
❑   Use of matching. (38; Fig. 4.3, 38)

❏   Experimental designs. (39–42; Fig. 4.4, 39; Fig. 4.5, 40; Fig. 4.6, 40; Fig. 4.7, 41)

❏   Deciding on the experimental design to use. (42; Fig. 4.8, 43)

❏   Length of experimental period. (58–59)

❏   Formative evaluation after the experiment has been implemented. (44–45)

❏   Collecting and analyzing data. (58–59)

❏   Writing the evaluation report concerning the impact of the modified program. (58–59)

References

Brainard, E. A. (1996). *A hands-on guide to school program evaluation*. Bloomington, IN: Phi Delta Kappa Educational Foundation.

Burns, J. M. (1978). *Leadership*. New York: Harper & Row.

Campbell, D. T., & Stanley, J. C. (1963). *Experimental and quasi-experimental designs for research*. Chicago: Rand McNally.

Costa, A. L., & Kallick, B. (Eds.). (1995). *Assessment in the learning organization*. Alexandria, VA: Association for Supervision and Curriculum Development.

Combs, A. W., & Snygg, D. (1959). *Individual behavior*. New York: Harper & Row.

DeRoche, E. F. (1987). *An administrator's guide for evaluating programs and personnel: An effective schools approach* (2nd ed.). Boston: Allyn & Bacon.

DuFour, R., & Eaker, R. (1992). *Creating the new American school: A principal's guide to school improvement*. Bloomington, IN: National Education Service.

Duke, D. L. (2006). What we know and don't know about improving low-performing schools. *Phi Delta Kappan, 87*(10), 730.

Fink, A. (1995). *Evaluation for education and psychology*. Thousand Oaks, CA: SAGE.

Fitzpatrick, J. L., Sanders, J. R. & Worthen, B. R. (2004). *Program evaluation: Alternative approaches and practical guidelines*. Boston, MA: Pearson Education, Inc.

Gredler, M. E. (1996). *Program Evaluation*. Englewood Cliffs, NJ: Prentice Hall.

Goldberg, M. (2005). Test mess 2: Are we doing better a year later? *Phi Delta Kappan, 86*(5), 389–395.

Hanes, J. C., & Hail, M. (1999, November). *New indicators for program evaluation*. Paper presented at the Annual Meeting of the American Evaluation Association, Orlando, FL. (ERIC Document Reproduction Service No. ED437412)

Hasenstab, J. K., & Wilson, C. C. (1989). *Training the teacher as a champion*. Nevada City, CA: Performance Learning Systems.

Jason, M. (1998). Perspectives on the principal's resolve as a factor in creating the quality school. In Y. Cano, F. H. Wood & J. C. Simmons (Eds.), *Creating high functioning schools: Practice and research* (pp. 21–28). Springfield, IL: Charles C Thomas.

Jenkins, J. A. (1993, April). *Can quality program evaluation really take place in schools?* Paper presented at the Annual Meeting of the American Educational Research Association, Atlanta, GA. (ERIC Document Reproduction Service No. ED397067)

Joint Committee on Standards for Educational Evaluation. (1994). *The program evaluation standards* (2nd ed.). Thousand Oaks, CA: SAGE.

Kellow, J. T. (1998). Beyond statistical significant tests: The importance of using other estimates of treatment effects to interpret evaluation results. *American Journal of Evaluation, 19*(1), 123–134. Retrieved August 8, 2006, from http://weblinks2.epnet.com

Krijcie, R. V., & Morgan, D. W. (1970). Determining sample size for research activities. *Education and Psychological Measurement,* 30, 606–610.

Leithwood, K. (1994). Leadership for school restructuring. *Educational Administration Quarterly, 30*(4), 498–518.

Leithwood, K., Leonard, L., & Sharratt, L. (1998). Conditions fostering organizational learning in schools. *Educational Administration Quarterly, 34*(2), 243–276.

McColskey, W., & McMunn, N. (2000). Strategies for dealing with high-stakes state tests. *Phi Delta Kappan, 82*(2), 115–120.

Monti, J., York-Barr, J., Kronberg, R., Stevenson, J., Vallejo, B., & Lunders, C. (1998). *Reflective practice: Creating capacities for school improvement.* Minneapolis Institute on Community Integration, Minnesota University. (ERIC Document Reproduction Service No. ED427470)

Owens, T. R. (1979). *Program evaluation skills for busy administrators.* Portland, OR: Northwest Regional Educational Laboratory.

Posavac, E. J., & Carey, R. G. (2007). *Program evaluation: Methods and case studies* (7th ed.). Upper Saddle River, NJ: Pearson Education, Inc.

Purkey, S. C., & Smith, M. S. (1983). Effective schools: A review. *Elementary School Journal, 83,* 427–452.

Purkey, S. C., & Smith, M. S. (1985). School reform: The district policy implications of the effective school literature. *Elementary School Journal, 85,* 353–389.

Roberts, C. (2000). Leading without control. In P. M. Senge, N. Cambron-McCabe, T. Lucas, B. Smith, J. Dutton & A. Kleiner, *Schools that learn.* New York: Doubleday.

Schmoker, M. (1999). *Results: The key to continuous school improvement* (2nd ed.). Alexandria, VA: Association for Supervision and Curriculum Development.

Senge, P. M. (1990). *The fifth discipline: The art and practice of the learning organization.* New York: Doubleday/Currency.

Senge, P. M., Cambron-McCabe, N., Lucas, T., Smith, B., Dutton, J., & Kleiner, A. (2000). *Schools that learn.* New York: Doubleday.

Sergiovanni, T. J. (1984). Leadership and excellence in schooling. *Educational Leadership, 41*(5), 4–13.

Sergiovanni, T. J. (1999). *Rethinking leadership.* Thousand Oaks, CA: Corwin Press.

Smith, M. L., & Glass, G. V. (1987). *Research and evaluation in the social sciences.* Englewood Cliffs, NJ: Prentice Hall.

Smith, S. (1996). Leadership training for cultural diversity. *MultiCultural Review, 5*(1), 33–38.

Sommers, W. (1995). Examining one practice as a lens to the whole system. In A.L. Costa & B. Kallick (Eds.) *Assessment in the learning organization: Shifting the paradigm* (pp.13-16). Alexandria, VA: Association for Supervision and Curriculum Development.

Stiggins, R. (2002). Assessment crisis: The absence of assessment for learning. *Phi Delta Kappan 83*(10), 758–765.

Stiggins, R. (2004). New assessment beliefs for a new school mission. *Phi Delta Kappan, 86*(1), 22–27.

Suter, W. N. (1998). *Primer of educational research.* Boston: Allyn & Bacon.

Urdan, T. C. (2005). *Statistics in plain English.* Mahwah, NJ: Lawrence Erlbaum.

Vaughan, E. D. (1998). *Statistics: Tools for understanding data in the behavioral sciences.* Upper Saddle River, NJ: Prentice Hall.

Weiss, C. H. (1998). *Evaluation.* Upper Saddle River, NJ: Prentice Hall.

Wiggins, G. (1996). Embracing accountability. *New Schools, New Communities, 12*(2), 4–10.

Index

CORWIN PRESS

The Corwin Press logo—a raven striding across an open book—represents the uni⋯ courage and learning. Corwin Press is committed to improving education for all learne⋯ publishing books and other professional development resources for those serving the fi⋯ PreK–12 education. By providing practical, hands-on materials, Corwin Press continu⋯ carry out the promise of its motto: **"Helping Educators Do Their Work Better."**